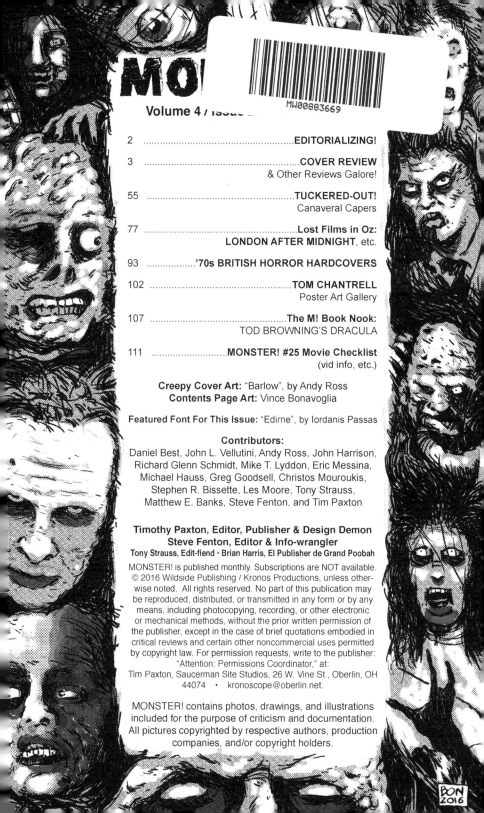

MO...

Volume 4 / Issue

Creepy Cover Art: "Barlow", by Andy Ross
Contents Page Art: Vince Bonavoglia

Featured Font For This Issue: "Edirne", by Iordanis Passas

Contributors:
Daniel Best, John L. Vellutini, Andy Ross, John Harrison,
Richard Glenn Schmidt, Mike T. Lyddon, Eric Messina,
Michael Hauss, Greg Goodsell, Christos Mouroukis,
Stephen R. Bissette, Les Moore, Tony Strauss,
Matthew E. Banks, Steve Fenton, and Tim Paxton

Timothy Paxton, Editor, Publisher & Design Demon
Steve Fenton, Editor & Info-wrangler
Tony Strauss, Edit-fiend • Brian Harris, El Publisher de Grand Poobah

BON
2016

EDITORIALIZING
SO, HOW LONG YOU BEEN COMING HERE?
By Brian Harris

When I started Wildside/Kronos with Tim, I had no illusions that we would be the next "big thang" in the indie/underground cine-zine scene, I just wanted to do us while giving others like us a chance to do them. Combining all of those wonderfully eclectic, eccentric, and trashy tastes into a magazine didn't just sound fun, it sounded necessary. We had to do it. I wanted to read something more than just horror, I wanted global cinema, exploitation, porn, fantasy, anime, sci-fi, action and anything else that floated our boats. People would be able to read our magazine and come away with at least one film they'd never seen or heard of before. I was consumed with the idea of becoming the go-to magazine for the odd and obscure, the kind of cinema zine that film nerds (like me) kept in their permanent collection for decades. I honestly believe we achieved that goal, but as months went on, there was something missing. Something uniquely...Tim.

Tim Paxton is an innovator and an artiste; he's the mad scientist of mad cool, zen master of zines. He is the most original guy I've ever had the pleasure of observing, and when you read one of our books, it is Tim's hands that guide you from top to bottom, left to right. His layouts pull you in and lead you along. You don't just finish a Wildside/Kronos publication...you reach the end of an unfairly short journey. People wanted more of that, more of what makes the man so engaging. Resurrecting *Monster!* wasn't just a logical move for us; it was a brilliant creative decision.

So here we are, three years into what I'd consider a modestly successful small-press publishing endeavor, and we've got a nutty quarterly and a kickass digest! Since *Monster!* dragged its way back to the land of the living, we've moved almost 15,000 copies. That's 625 readers, each and every month, checking out what Tim, Steve and the rest of the amazing writers in this mag have to say. Exciting, right? *[Wooo-hooooo! ☺ – SF]*

Seriously, I cannot imagine where we would be without the immense contributions of the writers that grace these pages. Without them, none of this would have been quite as enjoyable. Which brings me to another integral piece of this print machine: Steve Fenton. Accomplished author, unstoppable editor and engaging cinema superfan, Steve is just as much *Monster!* as Tim, and we're honored to be able to work with him every month. *[And I you guys, too – SF]* When you work with the *Monster!* team, you're working with decades of experience and, while it is daunting to be amongst giants, each issue is a learning experience.

So, what can *Monster!* fans look forward to in 2016? Well, for starters, more monsters, I'm hoping! With movements within global cinema to get back to old school, hands-on practical effects, we're seeing monsters take the spotlight in horror, fantasy and sci-fi once again. That means more

for us creature addicts and more for those of you out there reading through these pages for something unique, slimy and perhaps rubbery. Be they new or old, obscure or relatively well-known, *Monster!* is going to continue being the place to go for MONSTERS, and *only* monsters. The other guys—well—they'll jump on whatever is popular, milking the same old cows for those last remaining drops. We're going to push boundaries and keep things entertaining. Another reason 2016 is going to be really cool for readers...*MONSTER! INTERNATIONAL*. I know, I know: "Where the hell *is* it?!!" It's coming. *[Indeed it is! – Ye Eds]* Tim and Steve want this to be one of those unmistakably special releases that will knock your pants off. Stunning art, cool pics and comprehensive articles is their goal, and that's not something that can be rushed.

Three years and counting… Will we be here in five? Perhaps. Maybe. Okay, yeah: *absolutely*. Despite society's love affair with theft and their fascination with justifying it, support for what we do has never been better in the worldwide cult cinema community, and I only see that increasing with each passing year. We're getting word back from all over the world, from readers loving what Tim and Steve do and how *Monster!* continues to maintain a regular schedule at a fair price. Who would have imagined print could still get young people so excited? The responses have been surprising, and it's pretty satisfying knowing we have hundreds of regulars, just waiting with credit cards in hand for the next "ish". With this kind of growth, expect more Wildside/Kronos in 2016. So get ready for *Monster! International*, Tim Paxton's *Fantastic India* series and Troy Howarth's *Real Depravities: The Films of Klaus Kinski*. While we promise to remain as reliable as humanly possible, we also aim to keep things new and exciting.

In closing, I'd like to take a few words to express my gratitude to all of the writers that contribute to our fine publications. Each month you pour your heart and soul into your work and readers can feel your passion for the subject matter; your love for what you see makes them want to love what you love. I'm constantly told about readers hitting eBay or discount bins, and scoring hard-to-find films featured in the pages of *Monster!* Believe it or not, you are influencing readers and helping them explore new, and comfortable, avenues in cinema, and for that I am grateful. There was a time before the internet, when finding films often felt like an impossible task. You needed to belong to film clubs, purchase mags/zines and go to conventions. Along came the internet, and for a brief time finding films you might like to check out was a cinch. Then the information pile-on made it increasingly harder to decide in which direction to go when you wanted something that suited your tastes. People were told was bad was good, good was bad, everything sucked, everything was amazing. It's enough to discourage even the most determined film fans. Writers, keep helping the readers find their way—and Thank You.

Let Sleeping Vampires Lie: Barlow the Master (Reggie Nalder) is rudely awakened from his—*um*—beauty rest in **SALEM'S LOT**!

SALEM'S LOT

Reviewed by Andy Ross

USA, 1979. D: Tobe Hooper

The year was 1979.

Having grown up on a diet of BBC 2's "Horror Double Bills" and never once shrieked at the sight of a Dalek, it was a made-for-television movie that was to redefine my relationship with the horror genre. Having at that point not yet witnessed William Friedkin's **THE EXORCIST** (1973, USA) nor indeed John Landis' **AN AMERICAN WEREWOLF IN LONDON** (1980, UK/USA), the two-part screening of Stephen King's *'Salem's Lot*—the original novel's title comes with an extra apostrophe at the beginning, but it was dropped from that of the screen adaptation—was to print an indelible mark on my pubescent consciousness. As a 13-year-old monster fan living within close proximity of a cemetery and, for the first time, allocated a room of my own, to all intents I was the film's Mark Petrie character. With my bedroom walls adorned by dog-eared posters of Karloff and Lugosi, and my bookshelf buckling under the weight of my *Famous Monsters, Castle of Frankenstein* and *Tomb of Dracula* collection, like Petrie, whatever gaps were present in my knowledge of monsters probably wasn't worth knowing. One of numerous inhabitants of the New England township of Jerusalem's Lot, the story of Mark Petrie (like that of his mentor, Ben Mears) was to come to fruition in 1975. His second published work after *Carrie* (1974), *'Salem's Lot* (a contemporary take on the *Dracula* tale) was to reinforce King's unique style of storytelling. An earthy writer who took great pains to provide histories and anecdotes for his characters, reading *'Salem's Lot* for the first time was like being drawn into an alternative reality. The *SL* bug bit me in earnest in the summer of 1980. Taking a raincheck on the daily bike ride/swimming regimen that had become the seasonal standard, I had taken to reading King's novel during the lengthy school holidays. While it's true to say that the book and its contents were ahead of my intellect then, the raw experience of watching Tobe "**TEXAS CHAIN SAW MASSACRE**" Hooper's two-part production had left me in a state of awe.

Raising the bar for the vampire story, that *'Salem's Lot* was set in contemporary USA and that its heroes (in an age of reason) were everyday folks who could no longer depend on the trappings of faith to protect them, King's story was to realize an altogether fresh approach to the horror essay.

Following *Carrie* in the media transition from page to screen, *'Salem's Lot* (rather than being optioned as a feature film) was released as a two-part television series in November 1979. Produced by Richard Korbitz, directed by Hooper and adapted for television by Paul Monash, the $4 million production was released by Warner Brothers Television. With principal photography taking place between July and August of 1979, the series was shot against numerous locations in Ferndale, North ern California with additional interiors completed at The Burbank Studios. Whilst the process of turning a 427-page novel into a 210-page television script was to call for some sweeping changes (in particular to its characterizations), the finished product was as polished and as frightening as any big-screen shocker. Described by its author as *Dracula* by way of *Peyton Place*, whilst *'Salem's Lot* was very firmly set in the 20th Century, the story was to observe the more familiar trappings of the traditional Gothic horror. Proposing that evil can manifest in a particular location and that evil ultimately attracts evil, the focal point of King's story was the Marsten house, a brooding clapboard manor that overlooked the cosy Maine community of Jerusalem's Lot (hence the informal shortened title). When the return of Ben Mears (David Soul, from the TV cop series *Starsky and Hutch* [1975-79, USA]) coincides with the disappearance of youngster Ralphie Glick, the writers' concerns as to the inherent nature of evil very soon become apparent. Casting a terrifying shadow over the town's inhabitants, the arrival of antiques dealer William Straker (James Mason, from **JOURNEY TO THE CENTER OF THE EARTH** [1959, USA, D: Henry Levin]) and his "business" partner Kurt Barlow (Reggie Nalder, from **ZOLTAN – HOUND OF DRACULA** [a.k.a. **DRACULA'S DOG**, 1978, USA, D: Albert Band]) heralds a disturbing series of events. With its residents succumbing to a curious illness and modern medicine amiss of a diagnosis, the stage is set for an age old battle between the forces of good and evil.

Top to Bottom: Geoffrey Lewis gets it in the neck from newly-risen juvie bloodsucker Ronnie Scribner; *"Look at me!"* hisses Lewis repeatedly at Lew Ayres, hoping to hypnotize him; Barlow the Master, up close'n'personal; Father Callahan (James Gallery) goes faith to faith with the Master. Guess who wins!

A relative slow-burner in its first instalment, in true dramatic fashion, Hooper's adaptation increasingly picks up momentum. With much of part one establishing the setting and introducing the major players, it is only within the last 30 minutes that the more horrific elements of 'Salem's Lot creep in. Focusing on Ben's homecoming and his blossoming relationship with Susan Norton, the first part of the series similarly fleshes out its rich supporting ensemble. The sheer brilliance of 'Salem's Lot (both in its written and televisual representations) was to come by way of its down-to-earth depictions of its numerous inhabitants. A place of everyday folk whose routines very much mirrored our own, the unexpected appearance of outside interlopers provides a catalyst for the events that follow. The first of these new faces, Ben Mears, has retained very solid ties with the community. A silently strong and good-natured individual, as a young boy Mears had resided in the Lot with his elderly aunt Clara. Having moved away to the city and achieving moderate success as a writer, the recently-widowed Mears remains haunted by the experiences of his younger self. Forging a relationship with art teacher Susan Norton (Bonnie Bedelia, from **DIE HARD** [1988, USA, D: John McTiernan]) and reuniting with his former mentor Jason Burke (Lew Ayres, **BATTLE FOR THE PLANET OF THE APES** [1973, USA, D: J. Lee Thompson]), whilst Mears

secures a tentative foothold in the community, the disappearance of the youngest Glick boy places him firmly in the sights of police constable Parkins Gillespie (Kenneth McMillan, from **THE TAKING OF PELHAM ONE TWO THREE** [1974, USA, D: Joseph Sargent]). The second of these strangers, the aloof William Straker, opts to toy with the Lot's small-town mentality. Establishing a highbrow antiques shop in a locale well off the beaten track, Straker's enterprise—by its very nature—serves to attract the locals' attention. Projecting a cold and calculated charm, Straker is quick to establish ties with estate agent Larry Crockett (Fred Willard, from **THIS IS SPINAL TAP** [1984, USA, D: Rob Reiner]) who—having sold him both the Marsten house and the business premise—is keen to retain the patronage of the curt European. Agreeing to collect a consignment from the Portland Docks and employing Cully Sawyer (George Dzundza, from **THE DEER HUNTER** [1978, USA, D: Michael Cimino]) to undertake the task, Crockett deems to mastermind a liaison between himself and Sawyer's frivolous wife, Bonnie (Julie Cobb, from **THE SECOND COMING OF SUZANNE** (1974, USA, D: Michael Barry]). Unbeknownst to the dapper estate agent, Cully Sawyer has long harbored suspicions as to his wife's infidelity and, in order to catch the pair in the act, has subcontracted the work to plumber Ned Tebets

On the set of *Salem's Lot*, Tobe Hooper *[at extreme left]* directs vampirized kid Ronnie Scribner and soon-to-be-bitten grown-up Geoffrey Lewis, during the former's resurrection scene

5

(Barney McFadden, from the miniseries *Centennial* [1978-79, USA]) and gravedigger Mike Ryerson (Geoffrey Lewis, **THUNDERBOLT AND LIGHTFOOT** [1974, USA, D: Michael Cimino]). Collecting a cumbersome crate from the docks (i.e., the coffin of vampire Kurt Barlow) Tebets and Ryerson become increasingly uneasy in the presence of the shipment. Keen to get rid of the cargo, the pair hastily abandon the crate in the basement of the Martsen house. Failing to comply with Straker's strict orders to secure the shipment, the pair inadvertently expedite the horror.

Having been weaned on late-night screenings of Hammer films (often from behind a pillow and only partially observing the proceedings!), my first visit to *Salem's Lot* was to provide something of a revelation. Sat alongside a group of contemporaries (all of whom were determined to outstay the other), *Salem's Lot* was akin to a horror baptism by fire. With the shock aspect of the production augmented by its modern-day setting, the vampire as I had come to recognize

Top & Above: With his makeshift tongue-depressor cross at the ready, David "Hutch" Soul as hero Ben Mears reacts appropriately to a shocking sight in SL: it appears that Margery Glick (Clarissa Kaye) isn't quite so deceased as everyone thought...

it was no longer the preserve of a romanticized 19th Century milieu. Aware that vampires could exist as readily in the present as they could in the past—and it's safe to say that at this juncture I hadn't yet seen either **DRACULA A.D. 1972** (1972, UK, D: Alan Gibson) or **COUNT YORGA, VAMPIRE** (1970, USA, D: Bob Kelljan)—as a 13-year-old, I was genuinely perturbed by it. Embracing the new and far more visceral wave of American horror, *Salem's Lot* was a surprisingly vibrant take on the vampire legend. Owing as much to its ingenious casting as it did to its lavish production values, the two-parter was equally as rich in its spine-tingling episodes. As the first of these set-pieces (and one that was to set the overall mood for the production), the creepy revival of Ralphie Glick (whose capacity as sacrificial lamb serves to resurrect the Master, Kurt Barlow) remains one of its most memorable. Accompanied by the sound of repetitive low-key strings, the image of the ghoulish Ralphie floating towards his brother's bedroom window exerts a remarkably hypnotic effect on the viewer. Compelled to watch in spite of one's better judgement, the appearance of the youngster—all piercing yellow eyes and razor sharp teeth—was to leave a long-lasting impression. A similarly compelling scene, and one that consolidated the casting choice of former TV heartthrob David Soul, was the nocturnal reawakening of Margery Glick (Clarissa Kaye, from **NED KELLY** [1970, UK, D: Tony Richardson]). Having succumbed to the same sickness as her offspring, the death of Margery Glick presents Mears with a disquieting opportunity to prove his assumptions correct. Inviting Dr. Norton (Ed Flanders, from **THE EXORCIST III** [1990, USA, D: William Peter Blatty]) to join him on a vigil in the hospital morgue, the pair observe shell-shocked as the sheet covering the woman's cadaver begins to move. As she sits upright on the mortuary slab and inquires chillingly as to the whereabouts of her boys, Soul's reaction to the sight of her proffers nothing short of an acting master-class. Having already sold himself in the role and having exorcised the memory of Detective Ken Hutchinson, throughout his sweaty-palmed, faltering-voiced execution, Soul quite literally steals the scene.

Whilst stealing a scene is indeed commendable, stealing the show is something of a rarity. In *Salem's Lot*, that honor was to land in the lap of Austrian-born character actor Reggie Nalder. A performer whose distinct features (attributable to facial burns) achieved international note in Alfred Hitchcock's **THE MAN WHO KNEW TOO MUCH** (1956, USA), Nalder had a natural affinity for portraying quietly sinister scoundrels. A quality that brought him to the attention of acclaimed Giallo director Dario Argento, Nalder's appearance in **THE BIRD WITH THE CRYSTAL PLUMAGE** (*L'uccello*

Sans any special makeup the year prior (in '78), Reggie Nalder—billed under the alias "Detlef van Berg"—played a much-more-respectable character (Dr. Van Helsing, no less) in a far-less-respectable movie (the porno **DRACULA SUCKS**)

dalle piume di cristallo, 1969, Italy) was to set that reputation in stone. As the silent partner in the antiques dealership here, whilst the full reveal of Kurt Barlow is purposefully delayed until the second part of the production, when it eventually does happen, it's well-worth waiting for. Departing markedly from the description of Barlow in King's source-work, the **NOSFERATU**-like visage of Hooper's vampiristic villain was a deliberate ploy to avoid comparisons with Stoker's Transylvanian Count. A decision that didn't sit well with the author, that Barlow appeared so bestial (in addition to his limited vocabulary of growls and hisses) only added to the character's intensity. Stamping his authority on the proceedings in the series' most profound scene (a dramatic entrance that witnesses the vampire emerge from a black, shapeless mass before rising up to shatter the skulls of Mark Petrie's parents) proffers a pivotal moment in the narrative. With the youngster determined to avenge his parents and with Ben and Dr. Norton steeling themselves to confront the menace, the stage is set for a pulse-pounding finale…

As a sworn advocate of the horror genre and as one who has since witnessed far more visceral and psychologically shocking offerings, I can honestly say that *Salem's Lot* remains my personal favorite. Arriving at a time when the horror genre (thanks to Hooper, John Carpenter, and Wes Craven) was experiencing something of a revival, the miniseries was to show what could be readily achieved within the confines of television production. As one of a handful of King adaptations that have stood the test of time—which also includes Brian De Palma's **CARRIE** (1976), David Cronenberg's **THE DEAD ZONE** (1983), Rob Reiner's **STAND BY ME** (1986) and Frank Darabont's **THE SHAWSHANK REDEMPTION** (1994, all USA)—the distinct style of the author remains very much intact.

Given the makeover treatment in 2004, Mikael Salomon's (of the teleseries *Alias* [2001-06, USA]) take on the novel starred Rob Lowe as Ben Mears, Rutger Hauer as Kurt Barlow, and Donald Sutherland as William Straker. Whilst the remake adhered closer to King's manuscript (and included scenes that were omitted from Hooper's version), it lacked both the originality and shock value of its predecessor. With neither one what you might call a definitive adaptation, unlike Salomon's effort, Hooper's *Salem's Lot* remains a classic of contemporary horror television.

7

You don't wanna feel
THE LORELEY'S GRASP!

THE LORELEY'S GRASP

(*Las garras de Lorelei*)

Reviewed by Richard Glenn Schmidt

Spain, 1973. D: Amando de Ossorio

Tagline: *"You'll Never Sleep Alone Again!"*

One thing Amando de Ossorio did very well was give you a lot of bang for your buck, and this film is no exception. It combines gory killings, sexy ladies, a mythological creature, and a healthy dose of pseudoscience into a wonderfully fun stew as only the Spanish horror maestro behind the *Blind Dead* series could prepare for a hungry audience. My first viewing of this film didn't click with me, but one day, out of the blue, I just had to see it again. And again. And... *again!*

A German town is plagued by gruesome murders perpetrated by a lizard-like monster in a black cloak. Its razor-sharp claws dig into the flesh of nubile beauties, stealing their hearts for a snack; which is rather alarming, to say the least. The locals, especially the blind gypsy violinist (Francisco Nieto), say that a siren named Lorelei *[the more familiar Anglo spelling of the title character's name – ed.]* is to blame for these crimes. According to legend, she lives in the river and needs the hearts to live forever so that she can continue to stand guard over a vast treasure.

Elke (Silvia Tortosa), a teacher at the girls' school (read as: "grownup hot ladies' school"), tells the mayor (Luis Induni) that she is concerned for the safety of her students. He assures her that he has hired a master hunter to destroy the beast and this man will be guarding the school at night. What the mayor *doesn't* tell Elke is that this hunter is Sirgurd (Tony Kendall), a hunky dreamboat! With the schoolgirls fawning over Sirgurd like he was the last schnitzel in the Biergarten, Elke is pissed-off by his very presence. But it's only a matter of time before he melts her icy demeanor with his sheer manliness.

On his nightly rounds, Sirgurd spots Lorelei (Helga Liné) snooping around the grounds of the school. He gives chase but loses her, and more heartless victims keep piling-up. The next time he spots Lorelei, she's chilling by the riverside in her fringe

Contemporaneous US newspaper ad for **THE LORELEY'S GRASP**'s 1978 stateside release under a different title

bikini, being all seductive and stuff. Sirgurd is immediately smitten and, even with the evidence provided by the town's kooky professor (Ángel Menéndez), just can't believe she could possibly transform into a murderous monster by moonlight.

As his romance with Elke blooms, Sirgurd is also being beckoned by Lorelei to join him in her underwater castle lair to live for eternity. Well, eternal life for *her* anyway: his mortal ass will end up a skeleton like all her previous beaus. Armed with only some dynamite and the professor's radioactive dagger—which is pretty much all anyone ever needed to defeat anything—Sirgurd goes after Lorelei, her scar-faced goon, Alberic (Luis Barboo), and her green-skinned siren posse in leopard bikinis.

I'm so glad that I gave **THE LORELEY'S GRASP** another chance. Between the sexy ladies

A classic gimmick was reused once again for **LORELEY**'s retitled '85 Lightning Video release

and the flesh-shredding, rubbery lizard-hand of doom, I was just ashamed of myself for not bowing down before the statue of de Osssorio once again to pledge my unholy allegiance. His direction and writing are so on-point here; I mean, they'd *have* to be for a story this ridiculous! And few films are as steeped in the garish psychedelic fondue of the early 1970s as this one. The fashions and the décor have a war to see who can destroy the viewers' eyeballs first. Hey, guess what. *Both* sides win! *[As do we the viewers, too ☺ – SF.]*

German-born Helga Liné (in a thick layer of white pancake makeup) leads the charge of gorgeous ladies in **LORELEY'S GRASP**. She, Silvia Tortosa of **HORROR EXPRESS** (*Pánico en el Transiberiano*, 1972, UK/Spain, D: Eugenio Martín), and Loreta Tovar of de Ossorio's **THE NIGHT OF THE SORCERERS** (*La noche de los brujos*, 1974, Spain) are just three of the lovelies on display here. You tired of sexy women? You need some studliness? Look no further than Italian badass Kendall (r.n. Luciano Stella), of Mario Bava's **THE WHIP AND THE BODY** (*La frusta e il corpo*, 1963, Italy/France)! The scene where four of the luscious schoolgirls do their best to seduce him from the windows of the second floor of the school is probably the greatest cinematic achievement from the last century.

According to IMDb, International Cine Film Corporation picked up this film and released it as **THE SWINGING MONSTER** in 1976, but it was Independent Artists who distributed it under my favorite title, **WHEN THE SCREAMING STOPS**, in 1978 (for which barf bags were handed out to lucky viewers!). In 1985, good old Lightning Video released **WHEN THE SCREAMING STOPS** with some very misleading slasher imagery on the cover. The film got an amazing release from the now-defunct Deimos Entertainment in 2007. This DVD features both the English dub (which I prefer), the original Castilian audio, and an awesome essay by Mirek Lipinski about the film and where it stands in de Ossorio's filmography. There's a German Blu-ray of the film that I haven't seen firsthand, but I've read that it's a great release.

Be wary, my friends: Lorelei's blue hypnotizing stone may be too much for your mortal mind to bear! Do you hear that? That's the macabre laughter of the sirens as they contemplate your fate, which is likely an eternity chained to a wall in an underwater cave while the flesh rots off your bones. If you can hang with that, then I highly recommend **THE LORELEY'S GRASP**, a haunting and cheesy monster movie of the highest order.

THE LORELEY'S GRASP

A Hopefully-Not-Too-Redundant Second Opinion by Les "Slowpoke" Moore

As it turns out, coincidentally enough, both Richard Glenn Schmidt and myself happened to choose the same title to review this month. Since I had already started mine when Richard beat me to the punch and got his submission in first (you snooze, you lose!), and because I missed having anything in last issue, *Monster!* masters Tim P. and Steve F. took pity on me and were nice enough to offer to run my review anyway, on the condition that it didn't go over too much of the same ground. They said they'd edit my offering accordingly, so as to eliminate too much needless repetition, if any. *[No problem, Les. Having two enthusiastically positive appraisals of this woefully underappreciated cheeze cinema classic in the same ish is fine by us. Yours and Richard's reviews will hopefully complement each other – SF]* Having not yet seen what Richard has to say on the subject, I'll leave it up to the editors to decide what can stay in and what has to go. But, assuming he's already gone over the synopsis somewhat, I'll refrain from laboriously reiterating it here and simply give my impressions (etc.) of this old Eurotrash cinema favorite of mine instead.

As befits the title, the monster's lizardy maulers get lots of close-ups in **THE LORELEY'S GRASP**

I first saw this fabulous Spanish sexy shocker under its American theatrical release title **WHEN THE SCREAMING STOPS**, albeit not in a theater but under that same title on domestic home video back in the late '80s. It was love at first sight then, and I still have a soft spot for it now. What's not to like?! Even better, back when I first saw it as a rental tape on the old (1985) Lightning Video VHS back in the late '80s, it was in a sub-par fullscreen/pan-and-scan version. But that was then and this is now, and much more recently I scored a used copy of Deimos Entertainment's gorgeous 2007 domestic DVD edition, which was like seeing the film in a whole new light, in a pristine print at its full proper widescreen aspect ratio. *Damn!* Is it ever a fine time to be a trash movie freak! Okay,

enough of my gushing. On with the show...

As per the Anglo export trailer narration: *"A girls boarding school is living a nightmare. Who will be the next victim? [...] The monster stalks. Terror dominates their lives. The legend has turned into reality. Lorelei will be transformed into an obscene beast. She must devour human hearts in order to return to her centuries-old dream. [...] In order to live, it is necessary to kill. [...] A spectacular film with a chilling story of terror and death!"* (While the onscreen title reads **THE LORELEY'S GRASP**, curiously the much-too-understated narrator repeatedly calls it "**THE CLAWS OF LORELEI**" instead; this while that other title is clearly seen onscreen.)

In the film proper, a wandering Hungarian blind hippy fiddler/busker in blacked-out Lennon glasses (Francisco Nieto) forewarns the townsfolk, echoing some of the trailer narrator's words in the process: *"There will come new evils, I'm warning you. According to the tradition of the Seven Full Moons, Lorelei will be transformed into an obscene beast. She will need to devour human hearts in order to return to her centuries-old dream... There will be more deaths. Lorelei will need new victims. Many more victims."* (But do they listen to him? Of course not! And no prizes for guessing that he winds up a victim himself!)

The film wastes no time in cutting to the chase. Forget long, drawn-out scenes of plot exposition and character development, it gets to the meat of the matter right from frame one (and mighty meaty it is too, during the periodic splatter scenes, which, while repetitiously rendered, are surprisingly gruesome). In the prologue, on the eve of her wedding, a lovely young soon-to-be-bride (Betsabé Ruiz) is clawed-up real good (i.e., real *bad*) by some ferocious beast, right while's she's trying on her bridal veil, yet. After crashing through the window of her boudoir, the dimly-viewed creature proceeds to maul her savagely, leading into the opening titles. Other than for the fact that the perpetrator is obviously of non-human origin rather than a human psycho slasher, the scene might easily have come from any number of the Italo *giallo* thrillers being produced during much the same timeframe. Indeed, the bloodied, horror-contorted face of the freshly slaughtered starlet remains the focal point all through the credits, doubly immobilized not just by death but by freeze-frame as well (presumably simply because the actress couldn't have maintained the illusion of being dead for that long without moving and giving the game away).

Once again getting right to the nitty-gritty without stopping for coffee on the way, this camped-up and schlocked-out scenario promptly plonks down ultra-alpha male "Tony Kendall"/Luciano Stella ([1936-2009] best-known on the Continent as superduperspy Kommissar X) in an ever-popular and enviable sexploitation situation: as the sole fella in a building

Top to Bottom: An interesting expressionistic shot of the slashing claw-monster, seen as a blood-spattered wall;
Les sez, "If this is what yer average female water-demon looks like, by all means let 'em drag me to my watery doom"; and you thought acid reflux indigestion sucked! Never mind heartburn, in **THE LORELEY'S GRASP**, poor Ángel Menéndez gets half his face burned-off by acid; this is about the best look we ever get at the monster's mug: all of half of it for about half-a-second!

full of sexually curious young ladies! Appearing distinctly Elvis-like, he is first seen wearing painted-on jeans (with shamelessly accentuated frontal bulge) while being ogled lustfully by a bevy of jiggly, giggly bikini babes as he dismounts his motorbike toting a naked rifle ("open carry" nuts only wish they could look so effortlessly cool as him!). As a hunksome hunter named Sigurd, the sharp-dressed star—a real clothes horse who sports a new "hip" outfit for virtually *every* scene in which he appears—gets assigned to keep an eye (*wink-wink*) on the aforementioned boarding school, which (I should hope so!) is filled to the rafters with precocious, estrogen-driven "teenage" girls (actually twentysomethings). Having been contracted as a round-the-clock bodyguard to protect them from having their hearts torn out by a hideous supernatural reptile-monster, naturally enough, he doesn't do a very good job of this until the final reel, or else there'd be no plot!

Just like the girls (well, *almost*), Kendall also does topless scenes, but unfortunately shows us his nipples a lot more than they ever do (which is only very fleetingly a total of about twice, if you're lucky. But there are several shots of dark and shaggy '70sesque pubic triangles [a.k.a. "bushes"] visible through semi-sheer knickers, for those that like that sort of thing). With a perfectly-permed 'do and sporting nothing but the height of casual chic throughout, for one sequence Kendall wears a loud red-print shirt with a teardrop collar and a brown suede leather pantsuit with flared pants (hell, he's probably wearing Hai Karate aftershave, too!). And how about that outfit following his next of many wardrobe changes: a white shirt with press-stud buttons open to the waist so as to show off his hairy torso, along with crotch-enhancing, vertically-striped grey sailor britches with about 8" flared cuffs. Man, does this dude ever dress to kill, or what?! How long can wholesome leading lady Silvia Tortosa—playing a sexually inhibited school teacher—possibly resist his macho-manly allure, you may well be wondering ("He's very impertinent," she protests to the headmistress with prissy primness while suggestively fondling her pencil. "He thinks he's Don Juan!" But methinks the lady doth protest too much, as ol' Willie S. might say [*wink*]).

But what better guy for the gig than this unwaveringly cocksure man's man with testosterone on top of his testosterone! "I kill the game as it comes into my sights," he brags proudly. "I don't wait to find out what it is." While—being little more than a walking phallic symbol—he always keeps his long gun handy, for a self-professed expert ("I've been in this profession since I was *eleven*!"), he can barely even hit the side of a barn, let alone something that can actually move out of the way...such as an ambulatory amphibious monster, for instance. This foul creature proves to be far-from-foul costar Helga Liné (whose paella horror movie appearances are many) in inhuman form, as the earthly manifestation of a sailor-devouring siren from Norse legend, assigned by her celestial father Wōtan (a.k.a. Odin, king of the Norse gods) to stand guard for all eternity over the amassed treasure hoard of the Nibelungen. "It is part of my second nature to devour human hearts", she announces casually, resigned to her fate. Due to the fact that she periodically transforms into a toothy

Lounge Lizard: Liné and Kendall share a quiet moment

monster by night, Kendall the fully-human hero takes exception to becoming Liné's life-mate for all eternity and ultimately dissuades her amorous advances with the so-called "Sword of Siegfried" (which is basically little more than a glorified dagger, albeit one infused with some sort of radioactivity that is harmless to humans but fatal to Lorelei).

No sooner has the studly Sirgurd treated the lovely-but-deadly Lorelei to her first ever kiss than she falls head-over-gills (*sorry!*) in love with him. Because she's an amphibian, she can't stay out of water too long or else she dries up—yes, even while doing foreplay (or is it afterplay?) with to-die-for Tony—so her faithful henchman Alberic (played by frequent Euro-western/horror big dude Luis Barboo [1927-2001], whose numerous credits include playing Caronte in Jess Franco's **THE EROTIC RITES OF FRANKENSTEIN** [*La maldición de Frankenstein*, 1973, Spain/France] the year prior to this) has to periodically dunk her in the Rhine to re-wet her whistle. When she finds out that a local know-it-all scientist named Professor von Lander has been researching a means of destroying her, Lorelei has Alberic give him a sound bullwhipping in his lab; which he might actually have survived if he hadn't accidentally tipped over a flask of fast-acting acid on himself and melted his own face off (facial disfigurement via highly corrosive chemicals seems to be a bit of a pet motif of de Ossorio's, as Jack Taylor bought the farm in a similar manner in **THE NIGHT OF THE SORCERERS** [*La noche de los brujos*, 1974, Spain], which the director made following his next film post-**LORELEY**, namely **HORROR OF THE ZOMBIES** [*El buque maldito*, 1974, Spain], the second sequel to his best-remembered movie, **TOMBS OF THE BLIND DEAD** [*La noche del terror ciego*, 1972, Spain]).

And so to the fantasy milieu in which the hunky Sirgurd finds himself plonked: Unless the joint happened to be a cathouse rather than a schoolhouse, what's the odds that there'd be so many hot numbers all gathered together under the same roof! Assuming he or she swung that way, the casting director on this shoot must have had a field day selecting all its pulchritudinous female cast members from the cattle-call of starlets who likely scampered like bunnies in hopes of getting their "big break" by playing one of the many purely decorative roles seen herein. Kendall's primary love interest *señorita* Tortosa (who has a similar big-eyed, lush-lipped exoticism to her looks as her supersexy Spanielle colleague Diana Lorys, from Jess Franco's **THE AWFUL DR. ORLOF** [*Gritos en la noche*, 1962, Spain/France]; by no means a bad thing!) plays sultry schoolmarm Elke Ackerman, and her last name might possibly be an in-joke reference to Uncle Forry of *Famous Monsters* fame (but then again…).

Lissome blonde Alumna (Loreta Tovar, whose Christian name was here changed to the teasier "Lolita" for the occasion) has mischief written all over her from top to toe. While enjoying a late-night, stress-relieving bubble bath, for which one of her school-chums comes in to "platonically" scrub her back—no, she *doesn't* get nude and jump in the tub with her, you pervs!—who should come bursting in on the two "scrubbers" but Lorelei the she-monster, once again reverted to her nightly bestial form and out for virgin's blood. Luckily for Alumna, she gets away with just some minor flesh-wounds when Sirgurd arrives to roust the monster from the premises with gun blazing. That very next night, our heroine Elke also almost comes a cropper at the claw-monster's raking talons, but she too is saved by the timely advent of her hero Sirgurd, who may not be able to shoot straight but sure as shit knows how to make a date on time. Elsewhere, in an endearingly cheeky cheesecake scene which could only have originated in the Sexy 'Seventies—it might easily be an excerpt from virtually any European sexcom of the period—as smolderingly smoky, striptease-style saxophone plays on the soundtrack, each from their respective bedroom windows, the girls all vogue at Kendall seductively while he stands winking up at them from the terrace below (with his cocked, locked and loaded rifle firmly in hand, natch).

As Kendall's secondary love interest, olive green-eyed goddess-made-flesh the aforementioned Helga Liné plays the title seductive swimming siren ("My legend must continue for all time!"). A kind of tailless, two-legged mermaid who while in human form is shown slinking around the riverbank in a tasseled bikini, tippy-toeing barefoot through the mud, she periodically becomes transformed into that twice-aforementioned "obscene beast"; a scaly aquatic monster (her rubber-suited alter-ego was presumably *not* played by Liné!) with a hankering for ripping out human hearts—especially those belonging to scantily-clad virgin boarding schoolgirls—during nights of the full moon. Her amphibious enchantress can only remain on dry land in human form while wearing a magic pearl necklace (!). Leave it up to Kendall to grudgingly consign Liné's tormented lizardy soul to Valhalla via the enchanted/radioactive lizard-stabber in the last act.

The pedantically Van Helsing-like Prof. von Lander was played by Ángel Menéndez, who was only in about his mid-/late thirties at the time but, judging by his grey wig, wire-framed, oval-lensed granny glasses and stick-on salt 'n' pepper goatee and 'stache, he is playing much older than his actual age.

His old-fashioned "Colonel Sanders"-style suit with ribbon tie looks positively archaic next to Kendall's happenin' threads (talk about contrast!). Having freely admitted to working on experimentation "which science would consider fantastic...against all the elemental principles of biology", we just *know* he's nothing but a red herring, as is shortly revealed to be the case. He's been experimenting with a chemical formula, which he at one point injects into a noticeably wobbly rubber "severed hand" to cause cellular mutation within its dead tissues. His injection combined with a fancy moonbeam light projector aimed in its general direction cause the hand to "regress" back to its primordial reptilian origins. This is how he explains Lorelei's nightly unsightly metamorphoses, and it all makes perfect sense to us (check your zoology books, doubters!).

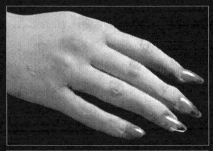

As per the title, we get plentiful emphatic close-up inserts of that scaly claw ripping the pulmonary organs out of its victims (which also include several males, so no calling the monster a "misogynist", okay?! Anyway, since the monster's female too, it wouldn't count, unless you happen to believe in that "internalized misogyny caused by the patriarchy" malarkey, that is).

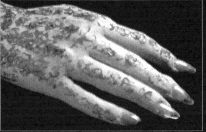

Although the bulk of the outdoor action as well as interiors were shot back home in Madre España, authentic Teutonic atmosphere is injected c/o plentiful inserted scenic views of mountainous Rhineland terrain (locations shot by seasoned old camera hand Miguel Fernández Mila, whose numerous other Spanish horror lensings include Ossorio's own first *BD* sequel, **RETURN OF THE BLIND DEAD** [*El ataque de los muertos sin ojos*, 1973]). A lurking, furtively peeping handheld camera sometimes represents the monster's POV. As for the soundtrack, while often sticking to classical motifs, seasoned composer Antón García Abril (who also scored de Ossorio's entire crucial *Blind Dead* saga) sometimes throws in some funky, Hammond organ-driven post-Mod "go-go" sounds that I bet Tony Strauss would love! ☺

And now for some background on one of the film's supporting cast members, who well deserves the longish paragraph I'm devoting to him simply because he's one of the many unsung heroes of European Trash Cinema (fondly known as "ETC" for short [thanks to a certain Mr. Craig Ledbetter]), with a long and impressive filmography as his legacy. I'm talking about late Italian-born/Spanish-based spaghetti/paella western stalwart Luis Induni (r.n. Luigi Induni Radice [1920-1979]). Even in some of his non-genre parts, he often seemed to merely be playing retreads of his stock western characters, as here. In **LORELEY**, Induni—as the distinguished mayor of the accursed

Top to Bottom: By means of a crude if effective stop-motion makeup appliqué technique (most of which occurs on a C/U of her hand), the lovely Lorelei devolves into something far less easy on the eye. For all its crudeness of execution, it's difficult not to love the ravening reptilian/amphibian monstrosity she becomes, and even though we don't get too many clear views of the monster—the camera mainly focuses on its scaly, flesh-ripping talons—it definitely gets its share of screen-time, so we can't complain, not with so many delectable starlets around to divert our attention during slower spots in the action rural German hamlet beset by titular bloodthirsty supernatural beast—essentially replayed his familiar sensible, trustworthily paternal sheriff part (w/ rifle). This was the kind of character he could walk through in his sleep by this point in his career, having played similar ones repeatedly in a great many Continental westerns, often of topnotch quality (e.g., "Anthony Ascott"/Giuliano Carnimeo's Gianni Garko *Sartana* outing **HAVE A GOOD FUNERAL, MY FRIEND** [*Buon funerale amigos!... paga Sartana*, 1970, Italy/ Spain], in which Induni played yet another in his long line of lawmen). Appearing in upwards of 50 SWs all-told, often in thankless, nameless tertiary roles for which he never even received onscreen credit, he was one of the genre's most prolific support players, and was usually seen as staunch "goodies". (Usual "baddie" the great Fernando Sancho was one of the few actors whose total number of western appearances topped Induni's; although, of course, the former's parts and billing—and most importantly of all, his pay packets—were considerably more substantial than the latter's were, him being a bona fide big name star and all.) Interestingly enough, for some reason Induni seemed to be cast (if not herein) more often as villains outside the western genre than within it. For instance, among his more offbeat castings, the actor played an atypical supporting character part in Juan Bosch's nudified possession thriller **EXORCISM** (*Exorcismo*, 1974, Spain), starring Paul Naschy. Playing one Udo Klein, the voyeuristic chauffeur of stately leading lady Maria Perschy, Induni lives in a seedy room decorated with nudie pin-ups and is ultimately revealed as a homicidal fanatic who commits suicide by leaping out a window rather than face his rightful comeuppance with justice. He also appeared under Naschy that same year in León Klimovsky's torturous historical drama **DEVIL'S POSSESSED** (*El mariscal del infierno*, 1974, Spain). The actor, a good friend of said horror star's, also appeared in the eighth instalment of Naschy's then-still-ongoing Waldemar Daninsky saga, Miguel Iglesias Bonns' **NIGHT OF THE HOWLING BEAST** (*La maldición de la bestia*, a.k.a. **THE WEREWOLF AND THE YETI**, 1975, Spain [see *Monster!* #8, p.49]). In the present film, while by no means villainous, if less like one of his unswervingly upstanding western lawmen than usual, Induni's character, who is evidently a bit of an old lecher, at one point openly ogles a bevy of bikini'd overaged "teenage" girls while they are cavorting in their boarding school swimming pool, remarking in surprise and apparent delight, "Whaddaya know?! I always thought they were so *skinny!*"

Speaking of the "skinny", here it is: not only does **THE LORELEY'S GRASP** give those that want 'em beef 'n' cheese aplenty in roughly equal amounts (if not much in the way of any real nudity, other than for a few fleeting glimpses of naughty bits here and there), but it comes with a satisfyingly gnarly, vicious monster and some grisly gore to boot, so it isn't completely bereft of entertainment value. Not by a long shot.

This shot of Helga as Lorelei is supposed to be her peering up from under the water, when actually it's the exact opposite, but it makes for a weird effect

Zombie ninjas strike with—*er*—**RAW FORCE**! They especially like to beat up on guys in PJs

RAW FORCE

Reviewed By Eric Messina

Philippines/USA, 1982. D: Edward Murphy

The first time I saw this flick (which has some of the *best* psychedelic "Martian/Barbarian"-style poster artwork ever!) was during an epic triple-feature courtesy of the dudes from the Austin Cinema Drafthouse (Zack Carlson and others) at the Castro Theater. The Castro was the best movie house, and I'm always weeping over the fact that I live in Tennessee now, so I can't go there anymore to check out "Midnights for Maniacs". That jaw-dropping triple-feature started off with **VIGILANTE** (1983, USA, D: William Lustig), followed by the present film, and was rounded-out by **LADY TERMINATOR** (*Pembalasan ratu pantai selatan*, 1989, Indonesia, D: "Jalil Jackson"/H. Tjut Djalil [see *Monster!* #21, p.35])! Out of those other two, this flick only half measured-up, but what it lacked in coherence it made up for in guffaws and wackiness. I mean, it's really unfair to even compare the three films—so I *won't*.

Force registers almost like a Filipinosploitation film written by the team who brought you *Three's Company* or *Fantasy Island*; it's trashy, sleazy and retarded, but lots of fun!

Originally I planned on reviewing it for my blog Theater of Guts (@ *www.theaterofguts.com*), but decided to bring it over to the faithful readers of *Monster!* instead. My buddy Skunkape procured a secret underground grey market copy for me three years ago that looked like refried shit, so I pined and waited, and now—thanks to Vinegar Syndrome—the world can enjoy this flick in pristine viewing condition! Obviously this was the reason why HD Blu-rays were invented: to showcase cult exploitation films from the Far East and elsewhere.

I know I've bashed VS in the past as a company that churns out SWV's sloppy seconds, but all that has changed, because they put *this* treasure out! They totally redeemed themselves (see, that's all it took to get on my good side!). Nothing about this flick says "Filipinosploitation", even though smiley Vic Diaz is prominently featured as one of the hooded island cannibals. Eddie Murphy is one bad-assed director, and he starts things off with a Hitler impersonator and naked female flesh. Oh Wait: it's the white Eddie Murphy, not the guy who never made another decent film after **COMING TO AMERICA** (1988). The way the hooded dudes cackle in super slo-mo while a Scot/Irish-looking blue-faced ninja in a Hawaiian get-up slices off female heads just screams that good times are about to happen! At least, *I* was overjoyed.

Cameron "penny-pincher" Mitchell is here too. *Ugh!* I've seen too much of him lately; I think I need to take a month away from his wretched pres-

The hair in **RAW FORCE** is way scarier than the zombies are

ence (may he rest in peace). Lloyd (Carl Anthony), a "Martuni"-swilling creepo, is a serial cheater along with a cast of martial arts enthusiasts off on a drunken sea cruise. And these are the characters we're supposed to identify with! Most of them look like an "After Hours" version of the clientele from the Regal Beagle. Most of the dudes wear ball-hugger (or "B's in a V") gym-shorts, and have droopy 'staches or comb-overs (maybe there's a power plant nearby?). There are tons of blonde babes to divert your attention away from the stink of machismo, though. As soon as slimeball Lloyd hits land, he dives into a cab and heads on down to the nearest cathouse. I like how his undershirt and polka-dotted underwear make him look like Bob's Big Boy!

The Hitler-impression guy (played by Ralph Lombardi) is following our heroes everywhere, always spying on them through binoculars. I like how they go from a whorehouse to a smoky all-nude dive bar where skanky girls squat-dance on the wooden bar as the foamy, pissy-looking beer flows tepidly. Even though I'm very sick of him, as far as Cameron Mitchell films go this and **THE TOOLBOX MURDERS** (1978, USA, D: Dennis Donnelly) are his best. The way he cackles and always wears a sailor hat makes me think he went to the Ernest Borgnine school of acting. Fake Hitler and a ponytailed bandana bro are annoyed that the good guys are on their way to Warrior's Island (which we saw in the beginning, complete with poor girls in cages and

Sadsack Attack: You call *this* sorry bunch cannibal monks and zombies?!?!

Vic Diaz). One bartender dude who looks like he could be in Sorcery, the band from **STUNT ROCK** (1980, Australia, D: Brian Trenchard-Smith) cracks a block of ice with his face! Another one who keeps bragging to everyone that he's a male stripper at the Stallion Galleon sadly reminds me of Tom Savini.

All the gratuitous female flesh and stupid antics really connected to my perpetual 12-year-old brain. This may be the best film in the VS catalog. It's *seriously* entertaining! Jim Wynorski (who was contacted via Facebook by the brain-trusts at VS) weighs-in on how he helped edit the finished product in an audio interview on the special edition DVD.

I like how there's one bible-thumper onboard (with blown-out, raccoon-like helmet hair) who judges everyone by saying, "I'm in the Devil's den!" Jewel Shepard from **THE RETURN OF THE LIVING DEAD** (1985, USA, D: Dan O'Bannon) flashes her tits and kind of looks down then laughs at the absurdity. I wonder if she mentions this movie in her book? Camille Keaton, whose breasts look amazing, acted in this directly after **I SPIT ON YOUR GRAVE (**1978, USA, D: Meir Zarchi), and her role is basically a forgettable cameo in a toilet.

The fight choreography is pretty decent (nothing compared to Golden Harvest, but then few are of that caliber). The high level of testosterone flowing throughout this male macho fantasy flick might be more extreme than the that seen in the **HEAVY METAL** cartoon (1981, Canada, D: Gerald Potterton), and I think of that one as the apex of the form. The cannibal monks don't make another appearance until the last 20 minutes, and there are hardly any monsters shown (they're more insinuated). The monks invoke the living dead to rise up over a pile of bloody meat and bones. Maybe they stopped off at the local BBQ joint for the gore effects—don't forget the Texas toast and wet naps! They show the zombie in super slo-mo again (I guess they were not drunk enough to stumble around like proper gut-munchers should). Talk about sad-sack zombies! These guys make the infected shit-covered, machinegun-toting undead from Lenzi's **NIGHTMARE CITY** (*Incubo sulla città contaminate*, 1980, Spain/Italy) look good. Most of them scowl at the camera and all have blue-tinged **DOTD**-style makeup. In the light of day they do flips, and can bust out some shitty Dolemite-style hong kong phooey, though. The makers actually had the balls to end this film with "To Be Continued", which is hysterical because no plans were ever made to do a continuation. I really enjoy this film on a stupid level of goofiness, and its audacity to never rise above the level of total masculine dumbness is most admirable indeed.

BRIDES OF SODOM

Reviewed by Greg Goodsell

USA, 2013. D: Creep Creepersin

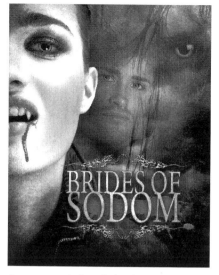

While the aforementioned title and following plot synopsis suggest porno, rest assured, **BRIDES OF SODOM** most certainly is not. And therein lies the rub…

Ten years after the apocalypse, after "nuclear missiles from all over the world were fired", the globe is plunged into impenetrable darkness. Vampires worldwide are coaxed out of their coffins under the cover of nuclear winter, and now enjoy being the dominant species.

The Lord of the Undead, Dionysus (Dylan Vox, wearing cobra-man facial makeup remarkably similar to the one seen in **DREAMSCAPE** [1984, USA, D: Joseph Ruben]) is in charge, with his Goth vampire sister Persephone (Rachel Zeskind) and his muscular hooded minions in black leather jockstraps. Bringing in some surviving humans for a blood feast, court boy Eros (David Taylor) falls in love at first bite for mortal Samuel (Domiziano Arcangeli). Persephone doesn't approve of the situation, as she craves Samuel for herself—and Eros and Samuel engage in some quick man-on-man sex with both their pants remaining firmly belted on. In response, Persephone then tries to engage in some lesbian sex with a mortal woman, but only winds up tearing the girl's throat out.

Narrowly rescuing Samuel from being turned into a vampire by Persephone, Eros and Samuel hightail it out of Dionysus' court. Eros then shares some backstory with Samuel on his current life situation: "I met Dionysus in a bar…" He then turns Samuel into a vampire! Go figure.

Bound and determined to get Samuel all to herself, Persephone learns of a pair of witches—annoying Goth girls who speak in free verse in unison, who are able to cast "anti-love spells"—and conspires with them to split up Eros and Samuel. Stealing a prized book of spells for the witches, Dionysus tells Persephone "You don't know how you've messed up!" The witches conjure up a scantily-clad, Medusa-like woman with snakes in her hair and big plastic boobies to do some interpretive dance moves before decimating the remaining cast with cheap video effects.

BRIDES OF SODOM is every bit as threadbare and ridiculous as it sounds. The majority of the film takes place in a singular set with grungy walls and wooden floors, with various bits of tatty décor for different scenes. The costumes are all straight from a strip-mall lingerie shop, and the gore effects are strictly joke store quality.

While the shabby production values and questionable acting suggests a cleaned-up XXX adult video, **BRIDES OF SODOM** is the work of bottom-level "auteurs" Creep Creepersin and Domiziano Arcangeli. This writer first became aware of Arcangeli from the elegantly-titled **HOUSE OF THE FLESH MANNEQUINS** (2009, USA), a no-budget production with muffled sound that is a shot-by-shot remake of Michael Powell's **PEEPING TOM** (1960, UK)! Arcangeli, from Italy, began his career as a teenage model for celebrated fashion photographer Helmut Newton, and has since forged a career in a series of curious straight-to-DVD horror titles: **VIRUS X** ([2010] also starring fellow "horror himbo" Joe Zaso and past-her-prime Sybil Danning), **THE GHOSTMAKER** (2012) and **SCARY OR DIE** (2012, all USA). As expected, none of these films are any good, but they make for compelling viewing for being very, very "off".

Existing somewhere between shot-on-video fan projects and Hollywood professionals killing a couple of spare afternoons, viewers

A dreadlocked vampiress from **BRIDES OF SODOM** shows off her dental work

with the actors gracefully trying to explain all the gaps in their résumés, are especially telling. As a lifelong Californian, this reviewer can vouch that these interviews are an accurate depiction of what Hollywood is *REALLY* like.

KEPERGOK POCONG

("Caught by a Pocong")

Reviewed by John L. Vellutini

Indonesia, 2011. D: Nayato Fio Nuala

of Arcangeli's features are left dumbstruck afterwards. Arcangeli's sole mainstream acting credit is in Sacha Baron Cohen's **BRUNO** (2009, USA), and Cohen's character in that film—about an Austrian fashion model who is essentially clueless—seems to apply to Arcangeli.

Calling to mind Tommy Wiseau's misguided vanity project **THE ROOM** (2004, USA), the films of Arcangeli remain fascinating for all the wrong reasons. A special treat awaits viewers who get **BRIDES OF SODOM** on DVD. Along with the expected behind-the-scenes footage and on-set photos, there is a series of interviews with cast members conducted by the incredible Dawna Lee Heising. (Google that name and be prepared to have your mind blown...) The interviews,

As is customary by now, I have to own-up to yet another egregious error that occurred in my article "Ties That Bind", the bulk of which appeared in *Monster!* #21 (September 2015 [pp.4-50]). Part 2, which included my errata/addenda, appeared in *M!* #22 (October 2015 [pp.102-108]). The review in #21 (on p.28) for **KEPERGOK POCONG** (*Caught by a Pocong*) is actually the review for **POCONG KESETANAN** ([*The Possessed Pocong*] 2011, D: Pinkan Utari). To correct this mistake and give the Devil (= Nayato) his due, I've decided to provide an accurate review of **KEPERGOK POCONG** in this issue.

Several college students hoping to make it big in the movies decide to expedite matters by filming a documentary on the everyday life of a gravedigger; a wise choice, as it turns out. Coincidental to this project, one of the two young men acquires a book entitled *How to Gain Fame and Fortune by Taking Photos of a Corpse Who in Life Had Lied While Taking a Pocong Oath and Then Been Struck Dead by a Pissed-Off God as Punishment* (I kid you not![1]). It should come as no surprise to anyone watching this movie that the very same graveyard attendant they're documenting is in the process of burying a corpse who, while alive, had lied while taking a *pocong* oath, and then been struck dead by a pissed-off god as punishment. Not wishing to forego this opportunity at fame and fortune, one of the youths videotapes the exhumed corpse, while the other takes a snapshot of it with his cellphone. This venture proves to be a successful one, as the young men not only experience a financial windfall, but are also offered roles in a movie. Meanwhile, the *pocong* decides to avenge

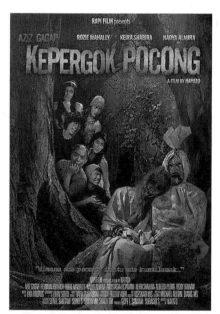

Indonesian poster

1 filmindonesia translates the title as *Tips to Get Rich Through Mystical Ways*. I like my title better!

himself on those who have invaded his privacy. The two men and the gravedigger soon find themselves victimized by hauntings, several of which involve a *kuntilanak*. Although the paper money acquired soon turns into fragments from a burial shroud, the two young men succeed in passing their screen-test dressed as drag queens. Emboldened by this success, the pair convince the gravedigger to exhume yet another corpse. Armed with cellphone and video camera and accompanied by a group of friends, they visit the prospective gravesite. As the proceedings are about to begin, the corpse plummets from the sky instead, causing the youths to scatter in panic. The gravedigger retrieves the reanimated woman's body, briefly dances with it, then carries it off slung over his shoulders.[2] The End.

I'm sure if I understood Indonesian I would have been laughing uproariously at the film's conclusion, except I don't and I wasn't. The ending is so abrupt—a common feature of many current Indonesian horror movies—and confusing that it left me scratching my head. Were it not for the frequent appearance of the *pocong*, this movie would have little to recommend it. At least **POCONG KESETANAN** also has the benefit of a hopping vampire (*jiangshi*), while **KEPERGOK POCONG** has only a sorry-ass *kuntilanak* to show for itself. In fact, albeit by another director, **POCONG KESETANAN** has the look (and smell) of yet another rotten effort by Nayato. The film even shares several cast members in common with **KEPERGOK POCONG**. Perhaps these two movies were separated at birth or shot back-to-back; perhaps Utari and Nayato attended the same film class in college and flunked-out together; perhaps—*Oh crap!* The IMBd informs me that "Pinkan Utari" is yet another directorial pseudonym of Nayato![3] This no doubt accounts for the fact that the film credits for **POCONG KESETANAN** conclude with outtakes from **3 POCONG IDIOT** ([*3 Idiot Pocong*] 2012 [see *M!* #22, p.108]), yet another steaming pile of excrement by that shit-shoveler himself. Somebody take a gun and shoot me!

As mentioned above, both movies share several actors in common, the most prominent being Aziz Gagap. Gagap is known for his "gay" caricatures, demeaning stereotypes endemic to Indonesian

comedi and *horor* films these days. Having seen him featured in four horror films by now—of which the most contemptible being **KAFAN SUNDEL BOLONG** ([*Kafan of the Ghost with a Hole in its Back*] 2012, D: Yoyok Dumprink)—his shtick grows wearisome after a while. If you should ever find yourself in Jakarta and see Gagap's name on a movie theater marquee, one should heed the admonition given in Dante's *Inferno*: "Abandon all hope, ye who enter here."[4]

KEPERGOK POCONG does possess one intriguing feature of interest. It reinforces the folklore belief that *pocong* signify good fortune. Like capturing a leprechaun in order to obligate him to show where his pot of gold is hidden, one should hug a wandering *pocong* to produce a similar result. Ever eager to further the ends of science, I decided to test this hypothesis by purchasing a set of three miniature *pocong*

4   As an incidental side-note to Gagap, the opening credits to **POCONG KESETANAN** list a cast member named "Febriyanie Ferdzilla"! I just assumed this was yet another alias that Nayato goes by. I mean, who in their right mind would name their child *that*?! Well, Febriyanie Ferdzilla does in fact exist; she is an actress who is featured in one of the better post-2000 Indonesian horror films, **JENGLOT PANTAI SELATAN** ([*Virgin Beach Creature*] 2011, D: Rizal Mantovani [see *M!* #21, p.28]). She even has her own FB page. Check it out!

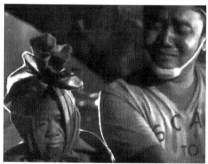

Top & Above: Aziz Gagap makes like a gay Lou Costello while repeatedly mugging at a shroud ghost in Nayato's **KEPERGOK POCONG** (2011)

2   The female corpse appears to be the *kuntilanak* featured in the film.

3   "Koya Pagayo" is Nayato's other alias, under which he has directed a number of *horor comedi*. As Pinkan Utari, *filmindonesia* lists ten other directorial credits to his name! I suspect that M. Night Shyamalan might be a pseudonym for Nayato as well.

off eBay from a woman named "Ladyhawk". According to Ms. Ladyhawk: "Your *hantu pocong* will whisper in your ear as you sleep, they will send visions of numbers into your dreams, and you will notice numbers here and there cropping up in your everyday waking hours—so please take note of those numbers—they are 'magic numbers' sent by your very own *hantu pocong* for you to use in lotteries, all forms of gambling, horse racing, and betting!" After being reassured that my new acquisitions would not "pester your pets", I decided what the hell and sent off my $25. I received my trio of *pocong* shortly thereafter, and they are now working their magic on the lottery tickets I purchased. Of course, I don't believe in any of that superstitious twaddle. Yeah, right. *Show me the money!*

Top: A starlet reacts to an unexpected apparition in **KEPERGOK POCONG. Above:** The highly un-monstrous Febriyanie Ferdzilla

GORY GORY HALLELUJAH

Reviewed by Greg Goodsell

USA, 2003. D: Susan Corcoran

Tagline: *"An Apocalyptic Fairy Tale."*

While the genre is becoming crowded, **GORY GORY HALLELUJAH** is a zombie slapstick comedy that few people have heard of. The zombies arrive in the last 20 minutes, but when they do, it's a remarkable sight!

Lensed in Washington State, **GORY GORY HALLELUJAH** has a lot on its mind and is wildly scattershot, best described as "The Greatest Movie Troma Studios Never Made".

Our story begins when four stage actors—bisexual hippie Sky (Tim Gouran), musical chorine Jessie (Angie Louise), angry African-American man Rahim (Jeff Gilbert) and nice Jewish guy Joshua (Todd Licea)—all audition for an insufferably pretentious passion play, *The Greatest Play Ever Written*. All four are auditioning for the part of Jesus Christ. Sky has a certain edge over the other three, as Jessie is a woman, Rahim is black, and Joshua, like Jesus, is Jewish. Those plans are dashed when the likewise insufferably pretentious director of the play decides to cast himself in the title role. Disheartened, our four thespians take to the road on motorcycles to audition for an East Coast revival in *Jesus Christ Superstar*.

The four can't keep out of trouble, and soon run afoul of a convention of Elvis Presley impersonators at a hotel. Forced to go on the lam after Jessie stabs an obese Elvis entertainer, our heroes end up in the conservative backwater burg of Jackville. Hauled into kangaroo court on trumped-up charges, the four are remaindered with certain townspeople until their case goes to trial. Sky is cloistered with beatific black sharecropper Mo Jack (Joseph Franklin), the one truly Christian person in town, who bears Jackville no ill will even if his entire family was slaughtered by them. Jessie is ordered to stay with Prudence (played by director Sue Corcoran), an outwardly prudish woman who secretly commands a New Age feminist cult. Rahim stays with the town's preacher (Keith Wilson), who also covers up

Zombies like to have spending money, just like the rest of us do. If only they could remember what to do with it

his intentions with a sanctimonious persona. He tells Rahim that Mo Jack's lands hide a magical talisman that will resurrect the dead, and makes promises to free him if he assists in his search. Joshua is sent to a brothel outside of town, where he falls hard for sweet, innocent shiksa hooker Mary Ann (Paige Green).

Slimy and unctuous real estate tycoon Ralph Peed (Jason Collins) enlists the aid of the townspeople, who wants to seize Mo Jack's land in order to build condominiums. At the climactic trial, held at the town's whitewashed church, all four actors are indicted on phony charges and the loving Mo Jack is denounced as a conspirator! As mob justice is meted out, Mo Jack's buried kinfolk erupt from their graves as horrifying zombies and rain down cannibalistic judgment on the hypocritical hillbillies in a series of hilarious, no-budget gore effects.

The work of the "Von Piglet Sisters", director Corcoran and screenwriter Angie Louise, **GORY GORY HALLELUJAH** has an awful lot on its plate other than gore effects. The film skewers both fundamentalist Christians on the right and New Age adherents and radicals on the left, but everything is turned aright at the end with all the characters resurrected and singing happy songs. Deliberately kitschy, all of the costumes are of the store-bought variety and the sets are crammed to the rafters with thrift store garbage. Satire sometimes doesn't work in film, as many viewers will see themselves as targets and walk away angry. Fear not, as **GORY GORY HALLELUJAH** doesn't have a mean

bone in its mildewing body. As if to assure the viewer that there are no hard feelings, all of the film's characters, good and bad, are magically resurrected at the end to sing and dance in a toe-tapping musical number. The main message it offers is to "love one another".

Never referenced in any books or studies on the zombie subgenre, **GORY GORY HALLELUJAH**, to the best of this reviewer's knowledge, has only been released one time and one time only on DVD, on the "Von Piglet Sisters" label. If you catch it in a used DVD bin, snatch it up. It's different— very, very different—and has a big, loving heart besides!

Who says a film all about love can't have homicidal zombies and bloody boobs in it?

UNDER THE BLOSSOMING CHERRY TREES

(桜の森の満開の下 / *Sakura no mori no mankai no shita*)

Reviewed by Eric Messina

Japan, 1975. D: Masahiro Shinoda

This Japanese release, whose screenplay was adapted from a story by Ango Sakaguchi, is very unassuming and, while not generally considered genuine horror or even a monster movie, I decided I must write about it for *Monster!* readers, because it has a "creature" scene towards the end that literally made my hair stand on end! I was completely caught off-guard by it. It all happened at 3 a.m., as I watched the film—which almost caused me to emit a silent scream of fright! You've been warned: *never* look up whilst under a cherry blossom tree…or you may never recover your sanity! This is the featured superstitious plot device, just keep your head down and look at the ground, which may seem ridiculous, but it totally works. That's the reason why I'm reviewing this unconventional arthouse flick by Japanese New Wave filmmaker Masahiro Shinoda, because it's a visually impressive tale of madness that hides one of the freakiest-looking creatures I've ever seen, which frightened me to the core.

I discovered this film through Hulu Plus and was intrigued, because it has Tomisaburo Wakayama, star of my favorite movie series, *Lone Wolf and Cub* (子連れ狼 / *Kozure Ōkami*, 1972-74, Japan). In that, he played the enigmatic Ogami Itto, a laconic wandering samurai on a trail of death and dismemberment, accompanied by his little boy Daigoro, who tags along in a well-armed baby cart. Wakayama acted in the present film just a few years after the series of six *Cub* movies had ended.

A child narrates the events of the cherry blossom festival, which is now considered a time for cheerful celebration, but a long time ago it was once feared as something that could cause madness and delirium. How could these gentle drifts of innocuously innocent pink flowers ever be considered menacing? (Oh, *you'll* see alright—*Mwhahaha!*) In Japanese culture, the symbolism of these majestic trees represents everything from the futility of life to kamikaze pilots who sacrificed themselves selflessly during WWII, or the spirit of renewal and rebuilding in the face of imminent death and destruction.

We meet Tomisaburo's character, a mountain man who wears a similar animal-skin-and-shorts combo to *Hagar the Horrible*, while robbing

The beauties of nature and the horrors of the supernatural collide in **UNDER THE BLOSSOMING CHERRY TREES**

and killing travelers unfortunate enough to venture into "his" part of the forest. He decides not to add an attractive female he meets to his long list of victims; which was a bad decision, because she quickly becomes a total drag, and even makes him lug her around on his back. My theory is that she is some sort of *Obariyon* (オバリヨン, or "piggyback demon"), a *yōkai* creature that forces people to give it rides on their backs, combined with the features of the *Masugami* (増髪, or "tangled-haired madwoman") mask from Noh theatre. She holds an unnatural power over his psyche, and he consistently listens to her out of simple bodily lust…and it doesn't end well for *either* of them. *[It is a Japanese art film, after all!* ☺ *– SF.]*

Obviously some sort of banshee or witch in disguise, this female devil (played by Shima Iwashita) holds the savage derelict mountain man's fragile will under her complete control. The first example of this comes when she gleefully instructs him to butcher all of his ex-wives (he has at least 7 of them!). Nothing he does can satisfy this spoiled, malicious manipulator, and he goes out of his way to do horrifying things that would only impress a psychopath, such as massacre random strangers for her pleasure. I like how the newlywed couple keeps one of the husband's wives alive for domestic servitude. Wakayama's character (who's never given an actual name) starts to hate the capital city, or what his new over-privileged bride represents. He seemed happier as a vagabond living off hunted animals and never combing his frazzled hair, but she pressures him into fitting into society by force.

By now you might be thinking, when's the monster gonna show up already!? This one requires patience, and it's more of a thought-provoking Japanese period piece that harbors a frightening payoff at the end. The flurries of cherry blossom petals begin to cause a hallucinogenic fear that affects the main protagonist. There are a few incidents with people running screaming in a paranoid frenzy once the leaves fall, but nothing prepares you for the vileness that ensues. Judge for yourself. Even if you don't think the gnarled being was as terrifying as I've made it out to be, you can still enjoy this as cerebral cinema. The horrific elements in this one are very subtle, and even though there's murder, manipulation and insanity, you can't really classify it as a horror film per se: but it is very psychologically disturbing, with evident supernatural elements. I don't want to give away the ending, but it's well worth sticking around for.

Japanese poster for **UNDER THE BLOSSOMING CHERRY TREES**

One very bizarre scene has the wife from hell using severed human heads as puppets, which sort of reminded me of the beginning of H.G. Lewis' **THE GRUESOME TWOSOME** (1967, USA). Wakayama's character begrudgingly assimilates into capital society, but of course, he's miserable. And what's worse is that his oppressive partner craves more severed heads. She acts like an immature necrophiliac and breastfeeds one of the decapitated victims, while the leftover heads begin to decay. She basically becomes a cranium junkie and hangs around their house making the bloody heads "talk" to each other for her own amusement.

Everything the former mountain man does is to impress a depraved lunatic who gets easily bored, and things become increasingly insane. When the withered, ghoulish creature is revealed, which I'm fighting the urge to describe in detail, even though this is *Monster!*; but I wouldn't want to spoil the big reveal. *[We were gonna run a picture, but decided not to. What better incentive for readers to want to see the movie! – ed.]* Let's just say that it literally gave me heart palpitations (even when I re-watched it for this review, I got all freaked-out again)! There's the notion that this vision may have been a psychological form of madness dredged up by the mountain man, and I wondered if he had indeed only imagined this demonic threat that may not ever have existed, except in his own mind. The film is very nihilistic, and there's no one really to identify with, just a nasty, foul ghoul lurking around the corner waiting to give you the shock of your life, and a maniacal mountain man who I felt slightly sorry for.

If you're expecting a samurai flick teeming with ghosts and witches, then you'll be disappointed, and the pacing is a little sluggish, but I'm reviewing this film for the one demon that scared me more than a whole stack of monster movies could, and because this folklorish Edo era tale of madness, manipulation and severed heads really crawled underneath my skin.

KING OF THE ZOMBIES

Reviewed by Michael Hauss

USA, 1941. D: Jean Yarbrough

Promo hype: *"ARE YOU A ZOMBIE? If you can sit through this spine-tingling carnival of shrieks and howls without getting the thrill of a lifetime... you must belong to the living dead!"*

I struggled with writing a review about this film because of one unsavory fact: that fact being that it is overtly racist in its attitude towards African-Americans. Simple as that; but then again *not* so simple. I asked myself, should I write a review of it and submit it for publication and influence even one person into viewing this highly offensive film? That thought entered my head, but ultimately one truism kept running through my mind, and that was the fact that the past is something we must learn from; we can't simply erase or run or hide from it, we must address this past indiscretion and see how hateful, derogatory and dehumanizing racism both was and still is. So, rather than just turn a blind eye towards it in this film, I decided to review it anyway, for what it's worth. Racism is today still very much with us, and much anger and resentment lingers from decade upon decade of racial bigotry, and when we view a film like this, we can see how far we've come since those days. But it is also evident that some scars will never heal, because the past is always there for us to re-witness, and to see how low mankind has sunk at times in their efforts to suppress another human race. **KOTZ** is a groan-inducing journey through a dark, depressing time when a man and a woman were commonly mistreated solely due to the color of their skin.

This short (only 67-minute) film by the Hollywood poverty row studio Monogram was their

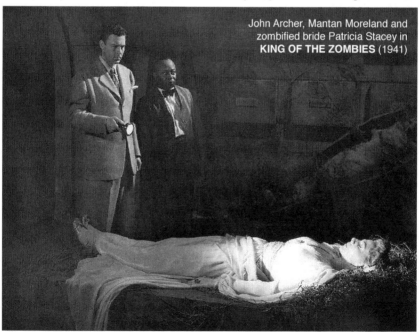

John Archer, Mantan Moreland and zombified bride Patricia Stacey in **KING OF THE ZOMBIES** (1941)

answer to—or "reinterpretation" of—the equally offensive, racist Bob Hope film **THE GHOST BREAKERS** (1940, USA, D: George Marshall), made the previous year. Of course, that RKO-produced Hope vehicle was a big-budgeted affair and did quite well at the box office, thus this much cheaper unflattering copy was made. In **KOTZ**, three men—two Caucasians, Bill Summers (John Archer) and James McCarthy, or "Mac", as he's called for short (Dick Purcell), along with Summers' African-American valet, Jefferson, a.k.a. just "Jeff" (Mantan Moreland)—are forced to crash-land on an unknown island (situated somewhere between Cuba and Puerto Rico) after their plane gets blown off-course during a severe storm. Upon crash-landing in a graveyard, of all places, Jeff believes he's been killed, but after being assured by Bill that he's not dead, he quips, "I thought I was a little off-color to be a ghost!" (This is only one of the film's non-stop barrage of race-related one-liners.) Out in the surrounding jungle, the trio subsequently stumble onto a creepy old mansion, whose owner Dr. Sangre (Henry Victor) is welcoming towards them, although his demeanor is decidedly sinister. Adding to the sinister tone, the only lights in the house are candles, which give a rather striking ambience to the proceedings. Right before they crash-landed in parts unknown, the trio had heard a mysterious radio transmission, evidently emanating from somewhere locally, but when they question Dr. Sangre about this, he replies evasively, "You must be mistaken. No broadcast from this island... *[your]* ears must have played tricks on you".

The castaways are led upstairs to their sleeping quarters by Dr. Sangre's gaunt manservant Momba (Leigh Whipper), who informs Jeff that, rather than remain with his white companions for the sleeping arrangements, he must spend the night in the servants' quarters instead, so as to "not set a bad example" for the Doctor's in-house menial staff. Bill and Mac are obliged to share a bed, but Jeff is led away to the kitchen, where we are introduced to an African-American woman named Samantha (Marguerite Whitten), who says she's from Alabama. An older woman named Tahama (Madame Sul-Te-Wan) stirs a bubbling cauldron, and smart-alecky Jeff jokingly asks Samantha if Tahama is "Methuselah", due to her advanced age. We learn that in reality Tahama is a voodoo high priestess, and is cooking up a magic potion intended to ward-off evil spirits. Samantha not only tells Jeff that the place is crawling with spirits, but she also mentions zombies, to which Jeff responds with "*Zombies?* What's them?" She further informs him that all he has to do is clap his hands and they'll come a-running (actually it's

Top: US one-sheet poster (art unsigned). **Above:** Note that Moreland's third-billed name is printed slightly larger than those of the nominal stars

more of a slow shuffle), whereupon Jeff does just that and two zombies promptly come lumbering in. Frightened by their appearance, Jeff hightails it up to Bill's and Mac's room, informing them of what he has just seen.

We are subsequently introduced to Dr. Sangre's wife Alyce (Patricia Stacey), who walks stiffly and stares blankly ahead in a telltale manner. The "good" doctor explains that the cause of her ailment is a strange malady for which he's trying to find the cure. Or might she perhaps have simply been placed under hypnosis by her hubby? It is never explicitly revealed what his national affiliations are, but to speculate that the doctor is garnering info for the Nazis would not be a bad guess; although, when this film was released (about seven months prior to the Japanese attack on Pearl Harbor), the United States had not yet entered into World War II, and was still officially neutral in the conflict. KOTZ's plot unfolds to reveal that a plane carrying U.S. Navy bigwig Admiral Wainwright (Guy Usher) had also previously crashed on the island, and that Dr. Sangre is trying to forcibly extract military intelligence from him to be dispatched back to the home country (presumably the Fatherland) via an elaborate radio communication device he keeps hidden in his basement. The doctor reveals to the marooned men that he has a fascination with occultism, as evidenced by the numerous tribal ceremonial masks and various other occult artifacts around his home. His niece Barbara (Joan Woodbury) also resides in the house. After she is caught reading a book on hypnotism by Bill and tries to hypnotize (or is it *un*-hypnotize?) her aunt, we can't quite figure out where her loyalties lie.

Mac disappears while looking for the shortwave radio set in hopes of getting an S.O.S. out as to their whereabouts, only to reappear after contracting some sort of dangerous jungle fever, which causes his death. Jeff gets hypnotized by the doctor and goes wandering about in a trance, still talking, obviously convinced he's a zombie, leading the other zombies—including revived living dead man Mac—around as if they were a squad of infantry in for dinner. Samantha notifies the addled Jeff that he's not a zombie, because he can talk, and when she salts his meal for him, she says, "If a zombie uses salt, he dries up and is dead again". *[A detail from Haitian* Vodou *belief which also featured in the 1966 Mexploitation zombie classic DR. SATAN (see* Monster! *#24, p.68) – ed.]* She also holds up a mirror and tells him that if he *was* a zombie, he wouldn't be able to see his reflection in it (vampire-style). After Jeff and Bill reconnect, they hear a scream and rush down into the basement, to there discover Dr. Sangre presiding over a voodoo ritual with the natives: a transmigration of their souls from Barbara and the captive admiral is being attempted, which our heroes endeavor to prevent...

KING OF THE ZOMBIES is saved by Mantan Moreland—its real "king"—as Jefferson. Even though he delivers dialogue that is obviously racially slanted at times, his comedic timing is excellent and his facial expressions are priceless. Moreland had a long and successful career in Hollywood. His CV also includes such films as the all-out comedy UP JUMPED THE DEVIL

(1941), the whodunit PHANTOM KILLER (1942, both D: William Beaudine) and yet another similar-themed horror movie, REVENGE OF THE ZOMBIES (1943, USA, D: Steve Sekely), among others.

Typically cast as heavies, as here, German-born actor Henry Victor has two films numbered among his 105 credits that particularly stand out for horror fans, those being Tod Browning's FREAKS and Karl Freund's Universal monster classic THE MUMMY (both 1932, USA). For that latter film, in which he played "The Saxon Warrior", Victor's scenes were cut out prior to its release, although (perhaps due to some contractual legality?) his name remains in both the opening and closing credits, at the very bottom of the cast list (his and a number of other scenes cut from THE MUMMY—"flashbacks" to different historical periods, detailing oft-reincarnated heroine Helen Grosvenor [Zita Johann]'s former lives—are now considered lost). On account of his German accent, Victor was cast as Nazis numerous times, and herein he plays an Austrian with heavily-implied Nazi loyalties. The great Bela Lugosi, whose career was already on the skids by this time, had originally been offered the Dr. Sangre role, but declined it due to having prior commitments (at the time he was appearing in other cheapies for cut-price outfits Monogram and PRC).

Dick Purcell, who gets top billing on this flick, has less screen time than Moreland and Archer. Purcell is best-known for his role of Grant Gardner, alias "Captain America", in the 15-chapter Republic serial CAPTAIN AMERICA (1944, USA, Ds: Elmer Clifton, John English); he died of a heart attack after playing a round of golf on April 10, 1944, at only 35 years of age.

Director Jean Yarbrough helmed some interesting films, including SHE-WOLF OF LONDON (1945), the Rondo Hatton classic THE BRUTE MAN (1946) and THE CREEPER (1948, all USA; see *Monster!* #9 [p.42] for coverage of the latter). Although actor John Archer registered as vapid in the present film, making for a rather boring lead (appropriately enough, he becomes transformed into a zombie), he does have some noteworthy "psychotronic" credits in his acting filmography, including Irving Pichel's DESTINATION MOON (1950), Fred F. Sears' ROCK AROUND THE CLOCK (1956) and Kurt Neumann's SHE DEVIL (1957, all USA; see *M!* #16 [p.46] for coverage of the latter).

As for KOTZ, it is a plodding effort that moves

at a snail's pace, making the short runtime feel much longer. The two Caucasian leads, Bill and Mac, are left with little to do, and sleepwalk through this low-budget affair. As I noted above, Moreland, a really fine comedian, steals the show (he was hugely popular not just within his own community, but with white audiences too, and was among the highest-earning black character actors of his day). Interestingly enough, while he is billed third in the opening credits, Moreland's name is printed in block caps a couple of point sizes larger than respectively first- and second-billed "stars" Purcell and Woodbury.

The minimalistic zombies in this film are afforded little more than a bit of dark shading on the cheeks to accent their cheekbones, and that's about it; they shuffle lugubriously along with arms extended and appear to be harmless... except at feeding time. However, their diet consists of soup—*not* human flesh!

KING OF THE ZOMBIES is loaded with many off-color references and the script is full of derogatory racial banter. You have been warned. Please watch at your own risk!

I Walked With The Zombies: Dick Purcell among the living dead

USA), **A CHRISTMAS STORY** (1983) and **PORKY'S** (1982, both Canada/USA) are all easily-recognized films, and **A CHRISTMAS STORY** has grown to become one of the most-beloved holiday films ever made.

But for me, Bob Clark is the dark force of nature who brought us the present film, as well as **DEAD OF NIGHT** (a.k.a. **DEATHDREAM**, 1974, Canada/UK), and also **BLACK CHRISTMAS** (1974, Canada), the '70s horror classic which—for better or worse—gave birth to the modern

CHILDREN SHOULDN'T PLAY WITH DEAD THINGS

(a.k.a. **CEMETERY OF THE DEAD**; **REVENGE OF THE LIVING DEAD**; **THINGS FROM THE GRAVE**; **ZOMBIE GRAVEYARD**)

Reviewed by Mike T. Lyddon

USA, 1972. D: Bob Clark (as "Benjamin Clark")

"Silence! The magnitude of your simplitude over-whelms me!" – Alan (Alan Ormsby) in the film.

While director Bob Clark may never have achieved household-name status in genre cinema, his body of work over the course of the last 40-odd years is quite impressive. **TURK 182!** (1985,

Alan Ormsby not only co-wrote and starred in the film, he even did the artwork for its poster, too

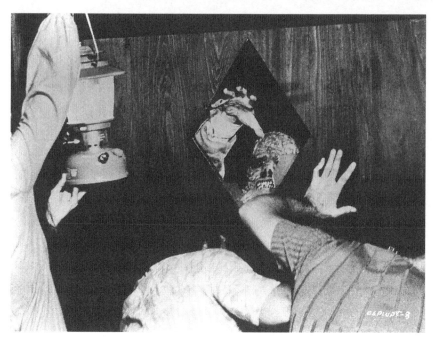

Momma done told 'em that children shouldn't play with dead things, but did they listen...

slasher film. I have a short list of horror films that really scared the hell out of me as a kid, and **BLACK CHRISTMAS** is on it! It was the almost supernatural presence of the killer tormenting his victims with some of the sickest, most gutturally disturbing, inhuman obscenities I'd ever heard in my life—spoken not by someone, it seemed, but by some*thing*: a demon waiting in the darkness, torturing his prey before killing them off in a variety of brutal ways.

This awesome shot of one of **CSPWDT**'s creepier zombies appeared way back in an issue of *FM*

BLACK CHRISTMAS stars John Saxon, Keir Dullea, Olivia Hussey, Margot Kidder and Andrea Martin, who would soon find her fame and fortune on the long-running Canadian comedy show *SCTV* (1976-84). What with that kind of powerhouse lineup of stars, it's hard to believe that a mere two years earlier, Bob Clark and Alan Ormsby had set out to make the cult classic low-budget shocker **CHILDREN SHOULDN'T PLAY WITH DEAD THINGS**. Working with a very modest budget of just $70,000.00, the duo's original plan was to make a cheap knockoff of **NIGHT OF THE LIVING DEAD** (1968, USA), but it turned out to be more than a mere attempt to cash-in on Romero's Pittsburgh-based masterpiece.

CSPWDT begins when an intrepid group of thespians lead by the often-amusing Alan (Ormsby) arrive on an island just off the coast of Florida in order to rehearse a play in the solitude of an old, decrepit house. Alan is a domineering, uppity little bastard who constantly reminds his campy underlings who's in charge. They all bow to his insufferable antics, but not without getting a verbal retort or two in just to even the score in typical regional theater fashion upon occasion. A hundred yards beyond the house lies an abandoned graveyard, and it's here that Alan brings his thespian cohorts in order to perform a "satanic ritual" with the intention of bringing the dead back to life. Naturally, the ceremony is unsuccessful (or *is* it?). Ormsby and the gang thereafter return to the house to get back to work…and that's when the *real* fun begins.

There are several things I like about this film: Bob Clark's campy script, the acting, the "remote island" setting, and a lot of the makeup effects. Sure, Clark and Ormsby set out to capitalize on **NOTLD**, but ultimately Clark came away with something rather unique in the zombie subgenre, whose influence is apparent in flicks like Dan O'Bannon's even-more-seminal, genre-busting classic **THE RETURN OF THE LIVING DEAD** (1985, USA).

The actors all work very well here, especially Alan Ormsby and Anya, his wife at the time, who plays the "supernatural sensitive" in the story, always channeling the vibe of the house and the eerie cemetery nearby with a glazed look of ghoulish glee.

And the graveyard: Rigged with just enough hard blue light and fog to create the optimal amount of creepy for the limited budget, the set was entirely constructed, from the fake headstones down to the crew digging through the shale stone-encrusted earth to make the graves. The modest necropolis takes on a truly foreboding quality which further enhances the scenes of the undead shuffling through the cemetery.

The zombie makeup effects are a bit of a mixed bag. Some are perfectly grotesque and disturbing, with a similar look to those of later '70s and '80s Euro efforts, while it seems like others were very hastily put together, with the end result being a look which seemingly says, "We're running out of time, so the rest of the actors had to do their own makeup". But considering **CSPWDT**'s micro budget, the zombies are overall very good, and they played a big role in the film's success.

It should be noted that Bob Clark made a two-picture deal at the time and ended up shooting **CSPWDT** and another low-budget classic, the aforementioned **DEAD OF NIGHT**, which was likewise scripted by Alan Ormsby. **DON** *[Which was in part influenced by W.W. Jacobs' classic 1902 short horror story "The Monkey's Paw" – ed.]* is an anti-war film about a young man

Orville Dunworth (Seth Sklarey) rises from the dead in this choice US lobby card from the film

Looking rather Frankie Monster-like, the highly photogenic Orville gets his big close-up in **CSPWDT**

killed in Vietnam who is wished back to life by his grieving mother, with terrifying results. It is a great little horror-drama, featuring many of the same cast from **CSPWDT**.

As for that latter film, I recommend the 35th Anniversary "Exhumed Edition" distributed by VCI Entertainment, which features a digitally-restored film transfer, a tribute to Bob Clark, plus a very interesting "Grindhouse Q&A" session with Alan Ormsby and assorted cast and crew.

While **CHILDREN SHOULDN'T PLAY WITH DEAD THINGS** might not be considered groundbreaking horror cinema, it is nonetheless a very entertaining slice of '70s sickness whose influence in later genre films of its kind cannot be denied.

LAKE PLACID VS. ANACONDA

Reviewed by Christos Mouroukis

USA, 2015. D: A.B. Stone

Dialogue quote: *"I'm not stupid! I watch reality TV!"*

Like it or not, the hard glam rock style known as "hair metal" was an important era for music, in many senses of the word. Despite how dated the whole thing now seems to be, the most successful of the hair metal bands had the most technically adept guitar players, they also had bass players who could play, they also had lead vocalists who could scream their heads off, they had drummers whose solos would leave anyone speechless, they had the best drugs and they had the doctors who wouldn't

let them die from the aforementioned drugs. Because of all the hairspray, lipstick and feminine clothing (etc.), many people doubted their masculinity (which was—*ahem*—important in the '80s *[Masculinity is* always *important, whatever the era!* ☺ *– SF]*). But the truth is that they always had the hottest chicks following them (including models and porn stars). *Why?* This would simply be because they made millions of dollars for themselves and for those around them (including managers and record companies). Where are those people now? Unfortunately they are stuck in half-empty clubs and revival shows with half the original band members missing because they either don't speak to each other anymore, or the whole thing doesn't make any sense economically these days, so they aren't interested anymore.

(Digression: Just for the record, since I started this whole "rock/movies" thing, I would also like to add that rock stars are typically *stupid*. I understand that some of them are talented and they write inspirational music or lyrics, but only very rarely do words of wisdom come out of their mouths when they open them in interviews. Which is absolutely fine; we shouldn't idolize *anyone*. Just because someone writes a song with which we can relate or identify, it doesn't mean that said lyricist represents our feelings in a spokesperson-like manner; because, if anything, we should at least have stuck to the whole "Kill Your Idols" aspect of the punk-rock manifesto. But please, don't quote this text in case you are ever caught going ape-shit, Charles Manson fashion.)

The state of affairs I discussed in the first paragraph is not so very different in the film industry. Similarly, back in the '80s, and to a large extent thanks to the VHS boom, many genre movie stars became as famous as rock idols; which is something that they desperately try to cling onto at fan conventions today. But the truth is, they usually end up in movies like the one under review...

Case in point Robert Englund, "Freddy Krueger" himself, who here plays Jim Bickerman, a handicapped old man who gets paid to help scientists whose actions result in the titular carnage. Ever wanted to see an anaconda fighting a lake? The title lake's monster crocodiles, I mean. Well, me neither, but SyFy thought we did, so that's what we get. Well, okay, I admit that I am a big fan of the *Lake Placid* films (**LAKE PLACID** [1999, D: Steve Miner], **LAKE PLACID 2** [2007, D: David Flores], **LAKE PLACID 3** [2010, D: Griff Furst], and even **LAKE PLACID: THE FINAL CHAPTER** [2012, D: Don Michael Paul], all USA), but I had not seen any of the *Anaconda* ones, so when this crossover vehicle was announced, I sat down and watched **ANACONDA** (1997, USA/Brazil/Peru, D: Luis Llosa), **ANACONDAS: THE HUNT FOR THE BLOOD ORCHID** (2004, USA, D: Dwight H. Little), **ANACONDA III** (2008), and **ANACONDA 4: TRAIL OF BLOOD** (2009, both USA/Romania, D: Don E. FauntLeRoy), as well.

As for **LAKE PLACID VS. ANACONDA**, don't expect a massive showdown involving snakes and crocodiles. You will indeed see a lot of bad CGI creatures in action and a respectable amount of blood will flow, but this is not the main attraction here. It is *the girls*. The synopsis on the back cover of the PAL Region 2 DVD that I bought clearly states, *"Packed with hot sorority girls, big guns, and jaws massive enough to swallow a human in one bite, this is one screaming good time!"* Now, please ignore those irrelevant guns and bites references and focus on the sorority girls instead, because—well—they get naked... often. As per usual, the film is set in Lake Placid (hey, check the title!), and this one is very generous in the nudity department. There are even many exploitative shots of butts, but I can't say I didn't enjoy them.

Other than that, the film seems to occasionally go off into parody territory, which makes sense, because after all, people would laugh *at* such things, so why not make them laugh *with* you at the moments you want them to? For a change, the screenplay by Berkeley Anderson (of **JARHEAD 2: FIELD OF FIRE** [2014, USA, D: Don Michael Paul]) contains colorful characters, although many of the ideas in it are half-baked, hence the whole thing feels rather like a Pete Shelley song: you know the inspiration is there, but had the material been worked by Axl Rose, it would have developed into something epic. *[No offense, Christos, but gimme The Buzzcocks over Guns N' Roses any day! ☺ – SF.]*

I was talking with a friend of mine (who is not a genre film buff, but is exceptionally well-educated and has a great knowledge of art, so his opinion counts to me) and he said that he cannot enjoy Dario Argento's films because he feels that there are moments when it seems that the auteur's intention is to scare the audience, but instead he provides—to my friend, at least—unintentional laughs. My immediate answer was that Argento never really had the means (i.e., enough money) to bring his otherworldly visions properly to the screen. I gave this quick explanation because, to be honest, to me Argento is the second-best director ever to walk on planet Earth (the first was Sergio Leone, and I'm not even talking about my favorites here—this is factual and objective, okay?), and I wanted to defend him and his work. We left the conversation at that, but this conclusion didn't seem satisfactory even to me. Why couldn't this friend of mine appreciate the King of *Gialli*? The answer came to me several weeks later (yes, I am slow like that): You have to understand the damn context! As an educated audience, we have to know when each film was made, in which country, by whom, under what intentions, under what political regime and social climate, under what damn budget and schedule, what were the other similar films within the genre, etc. There are of course two exceptions. 1) There will always be films that will be classics and will be easily appreciated by everyone, but "everyone" is a tricky word, so this exception mostly applies to major studios' successful baby-food (i.e., pabulum). 2) There will always be audiences that cannot be bothered to concern themselves with such background research, and I know damn well that they are the popcorn-eating majority, but I believe that those people are not readers of magazines such as the one you're holding right now. (No, not *Playboy*, the other one—*Monster!*)

Kindly study all those aforementioned aspects, and then you will see that it is impossible not to appreciate Argento's classics (please note that I am referring to his *classics*, just in case any of you want to bring up **GIALLO** [2009, USA/UK/Spain/Italy] and completely destroy my theory!). The above piece of thinking completely and appropriately applies to the film under review here, which you will only be able to appreciate for what it is.

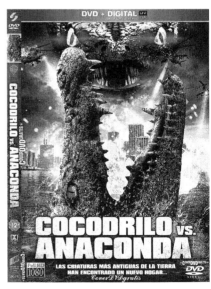

Hispanic DVD cover for **LAKE PLACID VS. ANACONDA**

WENDIGO: BOUND BY BLOOD

Reviewed by Greg Goodsell

USA, 2010. D: Len Kabasinski

Trailer ad-line: *"An Evil Returns To Wreak Havoc And Possess The Living."*

Say what you will about Tobe Hooper's **LIFEFORCE** (1985, UK/USA [see *Monster!* #12, p.9]), but it had the most radical reimagining of a space alien, *ever*: a beautiful naked woman, imperious to all that surrounded her. Coming so soon after the extravagant monstrosities found in John Carpenter's **THE THING** (1982, USA), the character and image of Mathilda May both excited and unnerved the male demographic for these types of films.

This concept is the best stolen idea found in **WENDIGO: BOUND BY BLOOD**, an amateur, no-budget feature found on lots of horror movie DVD compilations. The naked lady monster in this film (Deanna Visalle) is slightly worse for

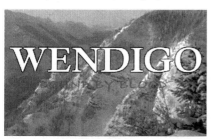

Top: The—*uh*—film's title card. **Above:** Props to Deanna Visalle as **W:BBB**'s supernatural slayer for prowling the wintry snowscape in her birthday suit...but was it really worth the effort?

wear than Mathilda, with a few tattoos, but she earns extra credit by stalking the countryside in several feet of snow! **WENDIGO: BOUND BY BLOOD** has all the earmarks of the shot-on-video horror feature: chunky gals, free-for-the-taking exterior sets, bad sound recording, worse acting. At least it's not yet another "found footage" film!

A definite "patch job," **WENDIGO** starts with a couple walking through the Pennsylvania woods tired, hungry and lost. After pitching a tent, the female part of this waylaid duo dies in her sleep, and her famished male companion reaches for a sharp object for a quick snack of "lady fingers". Not good, for as the introduction to the film states, anyone who partakes in cannibalism is hunted down by the wendigo, a malevolent Native American spirit that takes the form of a human to wreak vengeance. Nope, not really—that certainly doesn't resemble any version of the legend this writer has ever come across—but the woman comes back to life and kills her hapless companion anyway.

We then jump to the story proper: Small-town sheriff Craig (Brian Anthony) is investigating a crime scene when he meets Angeni Stonechild (Cheyenne King), a traveling Native American physician making house calls. Something's afoot, as people are turning up mutilated and half-eaten. Stonechild invokes the story of the wendigo, twice—once at the film's beginning and stapled somewhere in the middle. Never you mind, as this story is soon jettisoned altogether for a much more complicated crime story about two US Marshals being chased by a team of assassins in order to prevent their trial testimony against a crime boss. It is here that writer /director Len Kabasinski comes to the fore as the criminal gang's ringleader, with ponytail, attaché case full of weapons and attitude. The characters are chased around the wintry landscape. There are bad line-readings galore and naff shotgun effects, and those who originally signed up to see a horror film about a Native American spirit are left in the darkness, munching their popcorn in confusion.

Your humble reviewer has no knowledge about this, but it's a safe bet that Kabasinski started this off as a no-budget crime thriller, (probably originally entitled simply "**BOUND BY BLOOD**" before he disappointingly added "**WENDIGO**" to the title). He saw that the result didn't have the action or name stars to deliver to the audiences for that type of film, so decided to go the SOV monster movie route instead. The scenes involving the gang have very complicated

Tree-Hugger: The killer plant-monster twines its tentacular limbs around another of **LIVING HELL**'s pesky humans

split-screen effects and show a bit more care than the "horror" sections, which seem shot in a couple days with a camcorder. The overall effect is akin to the late Al Adamson, who would randomly edit crime thrillers together with monster footage in the hodgepodge manner of **THE FIEND WITH THE ELECTRONIC BRAIN** (a.k.a. **BLOOD OF GHASTLY HORROR** a.k.a. **PSYCHO À GO-GO** a.k.a. **THE MAN WITH THE SYNTHETIC BRAIN** a.k.a **ECHO OF TERROR** [etc., etc.], 1967, USA).

Kabasinski folded in scenes of the aforementioned naked lady possessed by the wendigo decimating a family (mostly off-screen, as the family includes a little girl, along with a trio of obese rednecks who turn into cannibals) and—*BANG! WALLOP!*—a horror film was made on the spot!

There is a new appreciation for shot-on-video horror films made in the 1980s circulating through the fan communities these days, but **WENDIGO: BOUND BY BLOOD** doesn't have the nostalgic allure that Chester Novell Turner's **TALES FROM THE QUADEAD ZONE** (1984, USA) has.

There are far better movies on this Native American legend, including director Larry Fessenden's aptly-titled **WENDIGO** (2001, USA). Catch that one instead of this, which will take at least a couple of decades before it's ultimately gifted with any campy, ironic appeal.

LIVING HELL

(a.k.a. **ORGANIZM**)

Reviewed by Christos Mouroukis

USA, 2008. D: Richard Jefferies

Ad-lines: *"Terror Takes Root... Some Things Shouldn't Be Disturbed... The military created it. An accident set it free. Now two people must lead us to survival... or extinction."*

What is it with the whole "Quentin Tarantino phenomenon"? Back when I was at film school, everyone was admiring him and they were always talking about what a genius he is. I wouldn't completely agree, because I grew up with the films he is "paying homage" to, so I was never impressed that much, nor did I ever think of his films as something all that original. But I also noticed that everyone was saying that Tarantino's strongest talent is the dialogue he writes. Maybe there's something original there that I hadn't noticed after all. I did some thinking over that: What exactly is the source of this dialogue? And the first thing that came to my mind was pulp paperbacks. It's not so difficult to put 2+2 together, because one of his most recognized works is called **PULP FICTION** (1994, USA), after all! The characters in his films talk like

35

¿ESTÁS PREPARADO PARA DESCUBRIR
LAS RAÍCES DEL MAL?

LIVING HELL

UNA PELÍCULA DE
RICHARD JEFFERIES
EFECTOS ESPECIALES DE
ROBERT KURTZMAN

Hispanic poster

them hilarious. It seems as if they were written by people who never saw an actual vagina in their lives. Or maybe this is just because they were specifically targeted at such an audience?)

But speaking of homages, another one I watched recently is the film under review, which screams **THE THING FROM ANOTHER WORLD** (1951, USA, Ds: Christian Nyby, Howard Hawks)—along with all its various derivatives, remakes and whatnot—as well as **THE BLOB** (1958, USA, Ds: Irvin S. Yeaworth, Jr., Russell S. Doughten, Jr.), again along with all the related films which came after it. As you may have noticed, both these aforementioned classics are sci-fi films from the '50s, and so the present homage is very similar to them in its tone and script.

LIVING HELL was written by Richard Jefferies (who also directed). Jefferies also produced the film with Gigi Pritzker (**ENDER'S GAME** [2013, USA, D: Gavin Hood]), Deborah Del Prete (**THE SPIRIT** [2008, USA, D: Frank Miller]), and David Greathouse (**TUSK** [2014, USA, D: Kevin Smith]).

The present film's story concerns one Frank Sears (Johnathon Schaech, from **QUARANTINE** [2008, USA, D: John Erick Dowdle]), who—as we are shown in a flashback to 1969—had some code-words and numbers scratched into his palms by his mother (Darlene Kegan, from **TWICE AS DEAD** [2009, USA, D: Terence H. Winkless]), who then killed her husband before killing herself.

they stepped out of the pulp paperbacks from the '60s, but pop culture followers rarely make the connection with things that were made so many years apart, hence Tarantino is winning Oscars. Is there anything wrong with that? Absolutely nothing; homage is important, and should be cherished. But, guys, seriously: original? (Incidentally, I recently started getting into '70s and [mostly] '80s porn paperbacks, and I find

Ooey-Gooey Badness: It's a **LIVING HELL**, but somebody's gotta do it

Back to the present: Frank now does a bit of research (the Internet always helps!), which leads him to the Fort Lambert army facility in Bennell, New Mexico, where, after he's denied entrance, he breaks in and miraculously doesn't get shot down by the trigger-happy soldiers. Once inside, and with the assistance of Carrie Freeborn (Erica Leerhsen, from **THE TEXAS CHAINSAW MASSACRE** remake [2003, USA, D: Marcus Nispel]), who works there, they discover a secret virus (Ms. Leerhsen bares her breasts—albeit only briefly—in one scene here, which you really have to see. Said scene is ridiculous, though, mainly for its context; which I sadly can't reveal, as it would be a spoiler). One thing leads to another and the parasite mutates into a creature that resembles a monstrous tree, which grows and spreads really rapidly, becoming a serious threat to our world...

This flick had an estimated budget of $4,500,000 and it was reportedly shot in 29 days in New Mexico, which is indeed a luxury when compared to the other Sci-Fi (or SyFy) Channel affairs that I usually review for the present magazine. For example, the cinematography by Eric Leach (**THE MAN WHO SHOOK THE HAND OF VICENTE FERNANDEZ** [2012, USA, D: Elia Petridis]) is stunning, especially in the outdoor shots.

They weren't called that back then, but my first engagement with social media was when I had two MySpace accounts (one for my films and one for my band, the nosferatu dot; lowercase letters intentional *[By all means check out their videos on YouTube, peeps! That's Christos behind the drum kit – SF]*). MySpace wasn't much of a social media vehicle to speak of, as seemingly everybody was there to promote one thing or another and personal profiles were scarce to come by. Later, when Facebook came to be, it actually started as a platform for university students to communicate with each other; and then it expanded to a network of actual personal profiles. But that changed soon enough, first with the creation of "groups" and then even more with the creation of "pages". It didn't take long for everybody to start promoting their businesses. Even old-school bands like Motörhead *[R.I.P., Lemmy! ☹ – SF]* have a strong Facebook presence nowadays. And let's not even get into all those "suggested posts"! People started sorting things out by either hiding things from their "timeline" or outright deleting people who became spammers. But how do you make $$$ in an oversaturated market? I have no idea, because I am not used to making money, but I suspect that

for you to make your product stand out in some way is a good place to start.

Such is the case with the movie under review here. Sure, there are a whole myriad of monster movies of its kind out there, but this one somehow seems...*special.*

LAVALANTULA

Reviewed by Christos Mouroukis

USA, 2015. D: Mike Mendez

"Could A Movie About Lava-Breathing Spiders Be The New SHARKNADO?" – Inside Edition headline (July 24, 2015).

Ad-line: *"Fire Burns... Lava Bites."*

The other day I came across an article that was probably written by some fundamentalist Christian of some sort or other, and she was shocked to discover how, in one of the *GTA San Andreas* games (I can't remember which one; I'm not much of a gamer), the player has the ability to fuck and kill prostitutes. And she was demanding that the game to be banned. Okay. People have the ability to fuck and kill prostitutes in real life too, and—guess what—they mostly don't, and we should not ban life itself because

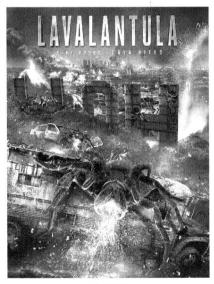

US poster

If a giant spider does this, run away real quick!

some assholes will do such acts. What we view is very important, but it is usually a reflection of who we already are. I mean, honestly, we usually watch films about people doing stuff. Or we even watch films about people doing nothing, as is the case with Jim Jarmusch's flicks (which I love nonetheless *[Hear-hear to that!* ☺ *– SF]*). Read on to the next paragraph...

I just finished reading Brian Harris' excellent book *filmBRAWL** (I like film guidebooks that keep it short and sweet, and don't shy away from the always-welcome humor; after all, this is *supposed* to be entertainment, after all!) and I noticed that, in his review of Andrea Bianchi's **BURIAL GROUND: THE NIGHTS OF TERROR** (*Le notti del terrore*, 1981, Italy) on page 87, he mentioned how some fans give heat to this zombie epic, because it is—admittedly—not as good as the rest of the era's Italian living dead affairs. You know, Brian is right in his observation, but I couldn't help but be a bit angry towards those aforementioned fans; and this is because we have become too spoiled (I hate myself for saying this...which it is a good thing!). And speaking of being spoiled, I have noticed that nowadays I rarely read a film book or magazine article and learn things I didn't already know. This may reveal my age, but even if I haven't actually seen the film under review, I still know what the writer is talking about. (One good exception is Tim Paxton's articles on Indian genre film, about which I don't know

jack-shit and therefore are eye-opening to me and a joy to read. I really admire a lot what Tim does with the subject. As for myself, I would never be able to do something like that. What I mean is that I really can't understand [let alone "read"] films that are foreign to the way I live. I almost exclusively consume media from the US and Europe. Even when the Asian ghost stories were popular in the early '00s, I wasn't able to give in, let alone get scared by them. I need to be part of the film's culture. I think it has a lot to do with my learning disability: I can read endless amounts of non-fiction [film journalism, etc.], but I cannot read fiction of any kind [well, I do read pulp porn paperbacks, but only occasionally]. This translates to film too. My main love in horror movies is violence from human to human. It is actually the exception for me the fact that I review these post-2000 monster movies for *M!*.)

Back in the analogue '90s, we—the evil hoarders—felt privileged for owning a third-generation VHS copy of such films, let alone an original copy, because these things contained scenes of atrocities we could get to see nowhere else! And guess what: we worshipped all of those films for that reason. Even the aforementioned **BURIAL GROUND** seemed like a masterpiece, simply because we didn't know any better, and that naivety was pure as driven snow. Now we own Bianchi's film on Blu-ray, for goodness sake...! Are we happier this way? I don't know, but a good thing is that nowadays, more often than ever, each film is reviewed on fairer ground, and it is usually judged based on content, rather than rarity (although, one way or another, sometimes "legend" status does color our views).

And based on content and taking into account the context, the film under review is excellent. It concerns famous B-movie actor Colton West (Steve Guttenberg, from my personal favorite **SHORT CIRCUIT** [1986, USA, D: John Badham]), who, amidst an exploding volcano in Los Angeles which pukes up gigantic lava-spiders that spit fire from their dirty great mouths, has to gain back lost trust from his disappointed wife (TV series star Nia Peeples, whose rack is amazing); oh yeah, and he also has to find his disappointed runaway son (Noah Hunt from **FLARE: THE HUNT** [2012, USA, D: Dan Brown]) in the process.

This is essentially a vehicle for one-liners from Steve Guttenberg, made specifically for the Twitter-trending generation, and screaming proof of that is the cameo from Ian Ziering (from the *Sharknado* franchise [2013-, USA]) who says he'd love to help, but he has shark problems. Does this count as a crossover that connects all this crap into a universe similar to that of the Marvel films, I wonder? I should have known this would be molded so much in the shape of **SHARKNADO**, as I first became aware of it when an ad for it popped-up while

I was watching **SHARKNADO 3: OH HELL NO!** (2015, USA, D: Anthony C. Ferrante).

On a side-note, the other day I saw a politician on television saying something outrageous—it doesn't matter who it was or what he said—and then a couple of days later a celebrity said something unrelated but equally stupid (again, it's irrelevant here who it was and what was said). Those two events surprised me a bit, and they seemed like something extraordinary, because my everyday routine doesn't have time for boring trash like that. I was talking about those two incidents with Faye, and she expressed the same surprise, as in "Why do those people—'celebrities'—feel the need to express every bit of crap they come up with?" Coincidentally, I had a similar conversation with a taxi driver, who was wondering: "Why do they always speak up their minds?" I came up with a very simple explanation. The small shop around the corner puts up a huge sign to advertise its business. That's what it can do in order to attract more customers, and that's what it does. Accordingly, celebrities have the media. They go on television, they humiliate themselves, and they destroy their dignity and their pride, and that's how they sell tickets to their shows (etc.) or how they get people to vote for them again. But I digress...

Other people besides Guttenberg and Peeples you will recognize in **LAVALANTULA** are

What better way to stop a giant, flame-spewing volcanic spider than with a fire extinguisher!

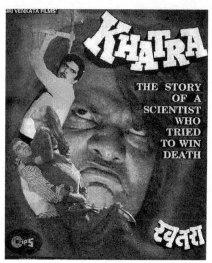

SRI VENKATA FILMS

KHATRA

THE STORY OF A SCIENTIST WHO TRIED TO WIN DEATH

टेवतरा

C195

Pressbook art for the Bollywood
Frankenstein film **KHATRA**

performers Patrick Renna (**DARK RIDE** [2006, USA, D: Craig Singer])—who gets to totally geek-out with his performance in the present film—and Ralph Garman (from the two *Ted* films [2012-15, USA, D: Seth MacFarlane]).

This was produced by Anthony Fankhauser (who was the line producer on the disturbing **I SPIT ON YOUR GRAVE 2** [2013, USA, D: Steven R. Monroe– *Weng's Chop* #5, p.154]) and it was executive-produced by Neil Elman (who also wrote the screenplay with Ashley O'Neil), Lisa M. Hansen (**STORMAGEDDON** [2015, USA, D: Nick Lyon]), and Paul Hertzberg (**ZODIAC: SIGNS OF THE APOCALYPSE** [2014, Canada, D: David Hogan]). **LAVALANTULA** was directed by Mike Mendez (**THE GRAVEDANCERS** [2006, USA]). A sequel is in the works even as you're reading this, and it'll be called **2 LAVA 2 LANTULA!** (2016, USA).

Personally, I'll be checking it out.

Editor's Note: Incidentally, to read an interview with *Monster!* publisher/contributor, *filmBRAWL* author and Wildside Head Honcho Brian Harris on the subjects of films, publishing, slasher flicks—which Bri mostly has no time for, as do(n't) we ye eds of *M!*—and beer (natch!), etc., check out Dan "Dante" Taylor's Exploitation Retrospect website (@ *http://www.dantenet. com/er/chats/interviews/wildside/brian-harris. html*). Loudly and proudly stamped *"NOW WITH MORE VULGARITY!"* right on the front cover, *filmBRAWL* is (to quote ER's Dante) a "bullet-stopping" 648-page *[!!!!]* paperback, further

described by its own publicity as a "genre cinema review guide featuring hundreds of encapsulated reviews and star ratings for those looking for a quick read on the toilet!" As of this writing, it was on sale at Lulu.com (@ *http://www.lulu. com/shop/brian-harris/filmbrawl/paperback/ product-14736108.html*) for the discounted price of only $26.56 (that's a savings of nearly a buck-and-a-half off the regularly listed cover price). So what you waitin' for, toilet-readers? Grab a copy, get on the john and get reading!

KHATRA

Reviewed by Tim Paxton

India, 1991. D: H.N. Singh

As similarly within their horror genre, in most Indian films with science-fictional elements, the "scientific accuracy" (if any) typically takes a backseat to all the wild dance numbers and excruciating comic relief mandatory to all movie genres. For the most part, efforts within India's SF movie genre have been less than thrilling, to say the least. But not all of the films were/are horrible, and from such examples as I have been able to see, these rarities, while sometimes interesting, are/were nowhere even close to being classics.

Interestingly enough, there is an odd sort of respect given to overachieving scientists in Indian cinema, even though their misguided actions may well border on insanity. Early examples of meddling—as opposed to all-out "mad"—doctors irresponsibly messing with things and powers they perhaps shouldn't be, includes India's first ever quasi-SF entry, **KHWAAB KI DUNIYA** (*"Dreamland"*, 1937, D: Vijay Bhatt), which is now considered lost. This "Invisible Man" film—which was probably somewhat influenced by Universal/James Whale's 1933 adaptation of H.G. Wells' novel, starring Claude Rains in the title role—was a musical comedy with slight sci-fi elements. Other pulp sci-fi efforts included a scientist creating monsters in the **KING KONG**-influenced **SHIKARI** (1963, D: Mohammed Hussain), as well as the B&W comedy hit MR. **X IN BOMBAY** (1964), director Shantilal Soni's super-silly but highly entertaining take on the invisible man subgenre. Sure, the plot is somewhat derivative of the aforementioned Hollywood take on Wells' classic, but, as with a lot of Indian films of that time, it has more to do with family intrigue, poetry, and love rather than dealing with any kind of true scientific issues. Director Soni had always dabbled in the fantasy genre, making films that dealt with loads of special effects, albeit done on-the-cheap. Soni's specialty was Mythologicals and fantastic Devotionals. **MR. X IN BOMBAY** is now considered a classic of Bollywood cinema, and was even remade by Vikram Bhatt (no relation to Vijay Bhatt, as far as I can tell), another director obsessed with special effects, whose recent feature **CREATURE 3D** ([2014] see *M!* #10, p.11]) was a fascinating dud. Bhatt updated the plot to his **MR. X** (2015), if keeping most of the lovey-dovey stuff, but instead of the poetry of the original, the film has more of a **HOLLOW MAN** (2000, USA, D: Paul Verhoeven) vibe to it, if minus all the rapiness. In **MR. X**, and our hero is a vigilante out to right wrongs and win the heart of a girl in the process (of course!).

These ambitious scientists almost always appear onscreen ineptly busying themselves in impossibly-overstocked labs full of colorful vials of bubbling liquids, humming machines with blinking lights and wires running from wall to wall. Even the more recent serious attempts at scientific accuracy have their labs resembling set designs from old Monogram or Republic serials of the 1940s and '50s. Typically, as in most such genre films (no matter what country they hail from), the scientist must either experiment on himself or, sometimes, whomever else just happens to be handy. While it's true that most of their onscreen experiments result in the doctor turning into something less-than-savory—as in **ZINDA LAASH** (see *M!* #24, p.102])—there have been fewer still Frankenstein-like undertakings which have resulted in man-made monsters.

Due to the sudden recent passing of actor Rajesh Vivek (who died this past January of a heart attack), I have decided to dig out one such film, called **KHATRA** (खतरा), in his memory. The word khatra is not that uncommon in Indian film titles. It means "danger" or "risk", and that pretty much sums up this cheaply-made Hindu Frankenstein tale.

Rugged has-been star Raza Murad stars as a single-minded scientist who is a respected doctor by day but an obsessed tinkerer with "things better left alone" by night. He is currently trying to reanimate dead human tissue; most notably a forearm that he has nicked from the morgue. His lab is full of the before-mentioned scientific types of "hi-tech" equipment (which is rather impoverished for a film made in 1991), and the experiment that commands his full attention is the severed human arm. Previous attempts to resurrect the limb have

resulted in failure, but he believes that tonight is the night he will finally achieve success. In a scene not at all unfamiliar to horror buffs[5], Murad attaches a few wires to the arm on the tabletop then attaches them to one of the beeping machines over on the opposite table. With a dramatic twist of a knob on his "fancy" equipment (!), Murad checks the timing of the electrical zaps on his wrist-watch. After giving it a few more jolts of juice, the limb remains motionless and lifeless. Murad then about-turns to fool around with some of his chemicals, in the process accidentally dribbling a "special serum" (i.e., some white gooey stuff) on the inert hand by

5 Hammer is full of such scenes, as is **THE FROZEN DEAD** (1966, UK, D: Herbert J. Leder), **FRANKENSTEIN: THE TRUE STORY** (1973, USA, D: Jack Smight), and many another monster movie containing quivering, abnormally-living body parts, which are typically seen suspended in vats of weird amniotic-type fluids, etc.

How To Make A Monster: *[top to bottom]* Mad scientist Raza Murad in his lab, full of all the traditional gadgets and vials. Having first revivified a severed arm using an electrode, the scientist later restores life to an entire corpse

It's Clobbering Time! Rajesh Vivek, who typically played *tantriks* or holy men in many of his films, is the resurrected Mr. Jackson of **KHATRA. Top to Bottom:** The newly-reborn monster is very childlike until he gets pissed, whereupon he stiffens-up, rolls his eyes back into his head, his black hair turns blond…and he is ready to go *berserk*!

mistake. Its fingers begin to move and Murad is overjoyed that he has at last accomplished his goal. The recently late Rajesh Vivek stars as Mr. Jackson, a slimy businessman who is admitted to the hospital following a horrific accident. His body having been crushed, he is seen lying in his hospital bed, swathed in blood-soaked bandages. He dies during an examination by Murad, whereafter his body is interred in the local Christian cemetery. Of course, this is all very convenient for the mad scientist, who witnesses Jackson's burial while hiding behind a nearby tree.

Meanwhile, the reanimated hand has gone a-wandering by its lonesome, and while off on a crawl nearby, who should it encounter but Murad's significant other. Luckily, while she is cowering in fear from the "attacking" forearm, the doctor returns home just in time to save her by simply picking up the errant crawling mauler and dropping it into a nearby trash can (!). Undaunted by the uncooperative antics of his recent renegade creation, Murad proceeds to revive his girlfriend, who had passed out on the floor from fright. He then shows her to the door, as he has "important" business to take care of… Since Jackson was Christian, he was not cremated as in the majority of Hindu burials. So, when night falls, the doctor sneaks back out and digs up the body.

Back in his lab, Murad lays Jackson's body out on the lab-slab. Whoever the mortician was, they did a splendid job on Jackson's mutilated body, as there is nary a mark to be seen on him anywhere, either form the accident or his autopsy. In fact, he is in remarkably fine shape, and the dude's hair is as near-perfect a stylish pompadour as one could hope for! The doc then sets up an I.V. drip, sending his special life-giving chemical concoction into a vein on the back of the corpse's hand, then attaches a couple of wires to its head and limbs, after which Murad switches on his apparatus and its eight little lights pulsate while emitting a series of beeping tones. Clearly some heavy Science shit is goin' down here! The doctor checks his wristwatch as the process slowly brings Jackson back to life. An eyelid flickers. Doc exclaims, "I have made it! [*fist-pumping the air triumphantly*] I have done it!"

Over the course of a few days, Murad teaches his new creation how to walk, catch a ball, and behave in a somewhat "human" manner. At this point it becomes obvious that Jack Smight's **FRANKENSTEIN: THE TRUE STORY** (1973, USA) partially provided the inspiration for Singh's film; including the runaway arm, the innocent and "beautiful" creature, and so forth.

It's not a direct rip-off of its partial inspiration source, like many other Bollywood productions are to a much greater degree, and Singh does manage to make the film his own, even while working with only very, *very* limited funds at his disposal. There was evidently little money for any special effects, and apparently even less-so for **KHATRA**'s monster. Watching this I was reminded of the "scar-free" look of other man-made monster movies, whereon financial restrictions made even the simplest of makeups seemingly impossible. A recent example was the monster in **GLASSHEAD** (1998, USA, D: Matthew S. Smith [see *M!* #17 and 18]), where there was talk of extensive skull reconstruction, but the operation left no lasting visible scars.

In **KHATRA**, our doctor leaves his creation by itself in the lab one night while he and his girlfriend decide to get frisky upstairs. Bored, the monster wanders around the house kicking his ball and drooling (he never speaks, but merely "acts" like a simpleton). He tries smoking a cigarette that his creator has left around, lighting one and taking a puff. Having discarded the burning cigarette in disgust, the monster proceeds to discover the amorous couple. "Monkey-see, monkey-do" being the order of the day, Jackson wants in on the fun, too!

The monster ignores his creator's demands to leave the room, and in anger his master strikes him. The confused monster steps backward, tugs on his lip in a deranged fashion, rolls his eyes up into his head (a classic "out-of-it" look that Vivek mastered for many of his *tantrik* roles), and—are you ready for this?!—his hair turns from black to blond. *Why?* I have no idea! I'm surprised that Vivek's brown eyes didn't turn bright green or blue, which is what usually happens in these films when someone is possessed by an evil spirit. Maybe contacts were not in the budget, so a change of wigs alone was in order. So from now on, this is how it goes: if his hair is black, he's okay, but when it changes to blond, watch out, because he turns into a "Euro-looking madman" (okay, that description was a bit of a long-shot, but it was all I could think of off the top of my head). The monster kills Murad and rapes his girlfriend, while the house, which has caught fire due to that carelessly discarded lighted cigarette, begins to fill up with smoke. The monster kills the woman, then, the house ablaze, he leaves ...

Meanwhile, somewhere across India, a wandering *baba* (i.e., holy man) is taking a pilgrimage across the land, visiting and preaching good ol' Hindu values to the poor folks he meets on his travels.

Crushed by a two-ton lorry, the monster grimaces and spasms as its life-giving goo gushes out of its broken body

During one of his rituals, he becomes aware that something is not right in the spiritual world, and that some sort of evil force has arrived on Earth. There is more to **KHATRA**'s plot (including all the usual subplots) about a vicious street gang, family issues, as well as the typical investigating police inspector character, but I'm going to skip all of the other malarkey. All that other action takes second seat to the monster plot, as far as I am concerned; but, this being an Indian film, such dramatic filler is what is normally expected by audiences.

Needless to say, the monstrous Mr. Jackson and the good *tantrik* eventually meet up, and the outcome is not pleasant. After a protracted tussle in a forest clearing, our monster rolls his eyeballs up into his forehead, goes "Super-Saiyan" on the holy man's ass, then finishes him off once and for all. The monster next turns his attention to the humans he once loved: his wife (played by Ektaa, a bodacious Bollywood hottie of the '90s)—who has fallen in love with the investigating police inspector since her husband's death—and the blind mother-in-law. Mr. Jackson arrives at their home and attacks them. In the process he wounds their dog which, true to its nature as the god Shiva's favorite animal, runs off like Lassie to fetch our heroic police inspector forthwith. Of course, once the dog arrives at the station and barks a few times, all is revealed, whereupon the hero rushes off to the mansion to save his beloved and her mum.

What I like about **KHATRA** most is that it is so *unlike* the Ramsay family's efforts of the period. There is no beast like in the Ramsays' **AJOOBA KUDRAT KA** or any ooey-gooey monster the likes of the one in Mohan Bhakri's **ROOHANI TAAQAT** (both 1991 graduates); indeed, nothing even remotely like those two creatures is seen in the present film. Also, while a *tantrik* does show up

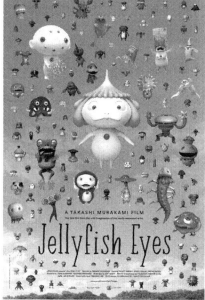

JELLYFISH EYES, from the original concept art *[top]* to the English poster art *[above]*

blank into its torso, either. All it succeeds in doing is pissing him off, as milky-white liquid oozes from the monster's wounds. The battling pair end up on the balcony and, as the monster rushes at our hero, the latter dodges out of the way, causing the former to plummet to the ground below, where the creature is run-over by a large passing lorry (i.e., truck) and reduced to a broken mass of flesh. White foamy liquid bubbles and sprays out of its wounds, as what remains of Mr. Jackson writhes in agony. After much gurgling and grimacing in his death throes, he succumbs to his wounds once again and dies for a second time. All is well, the two lovebirds are reunited and get married.

KHATRA is a pretty straightforward, no-nonsense affair, and chances are I would have missed it altogether had not a friend mentioned it on Facebook a few weeks ago. We were discussing the films of the recently-departed actor Rajesh Vivek and **KHATRA** came up in the same sentence as "Frankenstein monster". Okay! I have this film on VCD in my collection, but I had never gotten around to watching it till now. The cover made it look like a mad-killer thriller rather than a "Frankenstein"-type monster/horror film.

Singh's direction is not bad; he keeps things moving at a nice clip, with only occasional comedy relief intruding on the action proper. Had there been more to the budget, I don't doubt we would have seen something quite a bit different. The end result was helped immensely by the musical score by Aadesh Shrivastava (who also recently passed away), a composer credited on over 100 films who crafted a few toe-tapping numbers for **KHATRA**. But what really caught my attention was the background score for the film. There are a lot of funky electronic wails and basslines mixed with traditional sitar riffs and all sorts of other cross-genre soundtrack stylings mixed in. For all I know, he may have also composed the incidental music, or it may have been added later by someone adept at the kind of "cut-and-paste" scoring methods which were used on so many films back then. Whatever's the case, the soundtrack added to rather than detracted from my overall enjoyment of the film.

As far as actors' performances go, Vivek handled the monster side of his persona fairly well, although I wish he could have added more of a sinister element to his portrayal overall. The "childlike" monster-turned-serial-rapist/murderer could have been handled better if given more time and a bigger budget. Of course, these cheapo productions rarely had time for reshoots or extra takes, or even acting coaches, so far as I have been able to deduce. It was

for a few minutes, he is not the savior of the film. Instead we have a beetle-browed, stylishly-dressed undead killer that just so happens to go berserk. Typically, some Hindu god or other lends an assist in vanquishing the evil baddie, but not so in this film. Why? Is it because Mr. Jackson is a Christian monster? Not sure about that, but in the exciting finale it is neither the mighty Shiva nor Durga that comes to the rescue, but merely a lowly mortal officer of the law.

After a prolonged round of fisticuffs, our two combatants end up on the second floor of the mansion. Blow after blow doesn't seem to slow the seemingly invulnerable monster down any; neither does a few rounds of bullets fired point seemingly more a case of "We got three-grand and three days: let's knock this bad boy out!"

Ektaa (a.k.a. Ekta Sohini), who was discovered by Dev Anand in his 1990 film **AWAL NUMBER**, was in several other films at around the same time as she appeared in **KHATRA**, but she dropped out of sight shortly thereafter. Smalltime actress-cum-cabaret dancer Rakhsha Mehta likewise got a chance to show her assets herein. She also had a small role in Kiran Ramsay's **AKHRI CHEEKH** (another film made in the busy year of '91). Busty actress Huma Khan had the acting chops, but typically wasted her skills. She was a favorite of horror filmmaker Mohan Bhakri, and had bit parts or uncredited roles in numerous genre films, such as **MR. INDIA** (1987, D: Shekhar Kapur), **3D SAAMRI** (see *M!* #14, p.85]), **TAHKHANA** (1986, D: Shyam Ramsay, Tulsi Ramsay), and **KHOONI RAAT** (1991, D: Salim Hyder). Her career ended on an odd note: Kahn was arrested and convicted of kidnapping and torture of a young girl in 2012, and she is still behind bars as far as I can tell. Other than the usual pretty leading ladies, we have Sumeet Saigal who was the dashing police inspector, but, looking stern and concerned most of the time, he was given relatively little to do other than run around beating-up street thugs. Goga Kapoor appears as the holy man. He was in other genre films including the super-silly-but-fun Amitabh Bachchan action flick **TOOFAN** (1989, D: Ketan Desai), **AJOOBA KUDRAT KA** (a.k.a. **THE MAGNIFICENT GUARDIAN**, 1991, Ds: Shyam Ramsay, Tulsi Ramsay; see *M!* #3, p.51]), **BHAYAANAK** (1998, D: R. Mittal), **BHOOT RAAJ** (2000), plus a handful of action flicks

directed by Kanti Shah. He also starred in another film called **KHATRA**, a 1988 made-for-TV mystery thriller which—so far as I can tell—has nothing to do with our **KHATRA**.

All-in-all, I'm still managing to turn up obscure Indian monster films to write about, so don't think for a minute that you're going to get any kind of reprieve any time soon! ☺

[Special thanks to Mr. Subhajit Sen for his help on the preceding review]

JELLYFISH EYES
(めめめのくらげ / *Mememe no kurage*)

Reviewed by Tony Strauss

Japan, 2013. D: Takashi Murakami

This, the directorial debut of superstar Japanese visual artist Takashi Murakami, creator of the amazingly colorful and frenetic "superflat" hybrid style of fine art, may on its surface appear to be merely a family-friendly FX-driven fantasy film—and it is that, to be sure—but it is also a major example of the new wave of post-Fukushima Japanese cinema that has arisen following the horrible nuclear power plant disaster in March of 2011. Triggered by a devastating, earthquake-caused tsunami that struck the eastern coast, and exacerbated by a number of inexcusable failures in safety measures, the Fukushima Daiichi incident is the worst nuclear disaster since Chernobyl in 1986; it caused cataclysmic

Symbiotic Relationship: Kids and monsters go together like…well—*kids and monsters!*

One of master painter/sculptor Takashi Murakami's incredibly-intricate paintings, shown as part of his exhibition "In the Land of the Dead, Stepping on the Tail of a Rainbow" at NYC's Gagosian Gallery (November 10, 2014 to January 17, 2015)

change to the environment (and topography) of northern Japan, the ramifications of which are far-reaching and shall be long-suffered, possibly forever. With all the craziness that goes on in the Western world, it's easy to forget that an alarmingly large percentage of that country is still in shambles, still trying to rebuild and reorganize around newly-poisoned ground.

It is to be expected, then, that such a monumental disaster would affect the culture's artistic output, as well; art is one of the most fundamental and important ways we express ourselves as a species, in both good times and bad, and Japan as a culture has been dealt a tremendous blow, so it is only natural that we are seeing elements of their cinema take on a decidedly reactive tone. Much like the post-Hiroshima cinema of the '40s, '50s and '60s, for better or worse we are now witnessing a new cultural evolution of Japanese film from a country with fresh new wounds. There's much more to be said on this subject, but I'll have to tackle that in another article down the road in order to take a more thematically-focused look at post-Fukushima cinema. For now, I just wanted to give a little cultural context for the film under discussion, as it adds an important layer to a film that might be dismissed at first glance as

a mere family film. Though **JELLYFISH EYES** shouldn't be dismissed for *any* reason, not at all.

The story follows a young boy named Masashi (Takuto Sueoka) who, with his mother Yasuko (Mayu Tsuruta), moves from a government evacuation center to a small suburban town in the Japanese countryside following the death of his father during the Fukushima disaster. Despite the fact that both he and his mother are still completely devastated by their loss, they both do their best to keep brave faces for one another as they adjust to their new life in a new environment.

One day Masashi comes home to find their house ransacked and littered with the wrappers of his stash of Chee-kama (a processed cheese snack manufactured by the factory where his father worked), and is further alarmed when he discovers the culprit: a strange, 15-inch-tall pink flying monster with big adorable eyes and a cooing voice, made of 100% pure cuddle. Masashi sneaks the thing out into the woods and offers it a piece of Chee-kama, which it gleefully gobbles up. Masashi names the creature Kurage-bo ("jellyfish boy") due to the thing's semi-resemblance to a jellyfish, and the two quickly bond as they have a blast playing and horsing around together, Masashi being thrilled to have a friend.

The next day, in hopes of easing the stress of being the new kid in school, Masashi sneaks Kurage-bo to class in his backpack. Initially fearful of discovery, he is astonished to find out that every other kid also has a little monster playmate, which they all refer to as "F.R.I.E.N.D.s", each controlled with its own handheld touchscreen "Device"—something that Kurage-bo neither has nor requires. Every time the teacher turns her back, the kids all activate their Devices and cause their F.R.I.E.N.D.s to materialize. Masaki quickly learns that many of the kids pit their F.R.I.E.N.D.s against one another in battle, something he has no interest in doing, but when he is attacked by the class bully's F.R.I.E.N.D., Kurage-bo bursts to the rescue and proves itself to be a formidable fighter.[6] Masashi is befriended by a cute but forlorn girl from class named Saki (Himeka Asami), whose F.R.I.E.N.D. is the furry and formidably huge Luxor (who reminded me a little bit of the Muppets' Sweetums character), and the two of them, disgusted with fighting, vow not to use their own F.R.I.E.N.D.s for battle.

Meanwhile, we learn that in the town university's research center, a quartet of brilliant but unscrupulous scientists calling themselves The Black-Cloaked Four (Masataka Kubota, Hidemasa Shiozawa, Shota Sometani, Ami Ikenaga)—probably on account of the slick anime-style black cloaks the four of them wear—are hard at work on a top-secret project intended to use harnessed energy to control and prevent natural disasters such as earthquakes, but their mixture of super-science and ancient magic rites concerns their colleague Naoto (Takumi Saitoh), who also happens to be Masashi's uncle. Naoto was opposed to his sister and nephew moving to town, believing it to be dangerous—and it is: it turns out that the F.R.I.E.N.D.s are anomalous creations caused by the Black-Cloaked Four's energy experiments, which have been nefariously handed out to all the town's children along with Devices to harness the kids' negative energy caused by sadness, anger and fear and channel it to power their grand experiment. Though the project initially began with good intentions, it seems the power-mad BC4 have changed the direction of the mission to something bigger…and far more dangerous.

Nowadays, when you say a film is directed like an anime, it's no longer the novel and innovative style choice it was 10 or 15 years ago; it brings to mind hyper-stylized extreme angles and close-ups, amped-up action bordering on the superheroic, with backgrounds whizzing by like so many inked-in motion lines indicative of that cartooning style, and by now we have myriad frames of reference for this, attempted to varying degrees of success in live-action films. But when I tell you that **JELLYFISH EYES** is directed like an anime, I want you to think more along the lines of Hayao Miyazaki anime, particularly the likes of **MY NEIGHBOR TOTORO** (となりのトトロ / *Tonari no Totoro*, 1988) and **SPIRITED AWAY** (千と千尋の神隠し / *Sen to Chihiro no kamikakushi*, 2001, both Japan), with their wide-tracking panoramas, their beautiful quiet dramatic moments interspersed with sheer creative insanity, and their respectfully child-centric worldview and sense of wonder. This movie captures that kind of anime feel impeccably, even including some nice moments of the more traditional action-oriented aspects of the medium. Indeed, despite the many outstanding efforts to bring the anime style to live-action I've seen over the years, I've never before seen a film so natural and effortless at doing so, and without ever once feeling gimmicky about it. That alone makes it worth seeing for any fan of Japanese cinema, in my book.

Cuddlesome Critters: If these two stills above don't make you wanna see **JELLYFISH EYES** with your very own eyeballs ASAP, we dunno what else to tell ya

---

6   Interestingly, though it's never pointed out specifically by the film, Kurage-bo fights using Chinese kung fu, rather than Japanese karate, and at one point does a pretty amusing Bruce Lee shtick.

The so-called "**SON**" wasn't really related to the original **INGAGI** (1930) at all, other than by name. And check out that grossly misleading "artist's impression" behind the opening credits!

Add to that the fact that it's got a smart script with more than a few things on its mind—primarily, as noted earlier, its commentary on life in a post-Fukushima Japan. Aside from the disaster being the catalyst that sets the story into motion, with the widow and fatherless child uprooted and starting anew, as have so many disaster-affected Japanese citizens been forced to do, there are many other aspects of life in the newly-damaged Japan which the film touches on. Of course, the big one is the fear of earthquakes, with their prevention being the initial goal of the now-corrupted Black-Cloaked Four, but also the devastating potential of harnessed energy, the nihilistic concept of the destructive purge, post-nuclear health concerns, an overabundance of packaged foods and bottled water (and the ever-growing piles of their empty containers), the overwhelming feeling of sudden mistrust of a negligent system and the social ramifications that brings, and much more. This deceptively rich film is straining at the seams with its generous mixture of humanity and cultural concerns, while wisely avoiding any kind of heavy-handed "message moments" to bog down the fun of it all.

I'm trying to keep this all relatively vague so as not to spoil the discovery for you, as there is much to discover in this film. From the poignant sociopolitical commentary to the sympathetic characters to the full-force batshit crazy heights the story and special effects reach, this one is full of treasures, and never forgets to do the best thing a movie can do to us: fill us with wonder and joy. Don't even *think* about missing this one!

SON OF INGAGI

Reviewed by Steve Fenton

USA, 1940. D: Richard C. Kahn

Forget Jim Brown, Richard Roundtree, Fred Williamson, Pam Grier and Rudy Ray Moore. If you really wanna dig around and expose the deepest roots of Blaxploitation cinema, this makes a great (well, maybe that's too strong of a word; let's just say *good*) place to start...

Though there had been numerous earlier off-Hollywood B-movies made with (quote) "all-colored" casts (for instance, the dimes-on-the-dollar output of early African-American "movie mogul" Oscar Micheaux and the likes of the voodoo melodrama **THE DEVIL'S DAUGHTER** [a.k.a. **POCOMANIA** 1939, D: Arthur Leonard] *et al*) in the '30s, **SON OF INGAGI**—which is related to the original smash-hit roadshow attraction **INGAGI** (1930, USA, D: William Campbell) in name only; consider him the illegitimate offspring!—sticks to the strictly poverty row, PRC white-boy formula. In fact, it reads very much like an ebony take on one of that studio's or Monogram Pictures' creepy cheapies, if still more financially impoverished than the norm. Like those other monetarily-challenged production houses (which managed to keep the gravy train rollin' along just nicely for a time regardless, and handed us down some real low-budget gems for posterity in the process), this Sack Amusement Enterprises feature keeps its thrills strictly on the cheap, shooting locally in the nabe—right next door, in fact—rather than incurring unaffordable extra costs by going off on location or renting fancy standing sets that might at least give an appearance of exotic foreign locales. In my opinion, rather than being a detracting factor, this cozy, folksy homemade/"down-homey" tone really adds to **SON**'s charm, of which it has plenty for those willing to see it.

As for its namesake, certain reissue ads hyped the original '30 **INGAGI** as a *"Half Human – Half Ape Monster!"* That now-difficult-to-see (if not actually lost) film, from which stills, posters, snippets of footage and even the film's Vitaphone audio track (recorded on lo-fi 78 rpm wax records [it is posted in sections on YouTube]) are still readily extant, it no longer has any prints in active circulation, although copies of variable condition are known to exist in private collections. But restoration is costly and the profit margin for such a vintage "special interest" title would be small, hence it continues to languish in the vaults. Hopefully an intact print might turn up someday; possibly from Down Under, where other hard-to-acquire or lost films have been rediscovered over the years. As big daddy Ingagi in the 1930 film, future frequent Hollywood gorilla man Charles Gemora played his first ever of many onscreen apes, carting topless native women off into the African jungle for—*ahem*—mating purposes (some footage was allegedly shot on location in the jungles of the Democratic Republic of Congo, but in 1949, its distributor Dwain Esper was issued with a cease-and-desist order by the Federal Trade Commission, demanding that he stop claiming in advertising that it was shot in Africa, when really it was shot stateside. He also got in trouble with New York's Better Business Bureau for faking so-called authentic

As N'Gina, extra-tall Zack Williams carries the heroine Eleanor (Daisy Bufford) cradled in his extra-hairy arms

gorilla footage, and was also sued to the tune of 150-grand by a private individual for using some preexisting ethnographic documentary footage [shot way back in 1915] without permission). **INGAGI**'s alleged African "pygmies" were actually portrayed by a number of heavily made-up preteen black kids from the LA area, and a bogus "new species" of poisonous reptile called a "Tortadillo" seen in the film was merely a plain ol' tortoise enhanced with various artificial attachments (including a horn, scales and what was evidently an armadillo's tail). According to a thread at Monster Kid Classic Horror Forum[7], *"The title **INGAGI** was supposedly an African word for gorilla. No such word was found in any African language."* Co-billing it on the bottom half of double-bills with Tod Browning's oft-censored/banned 1932 shocker **FREAKS**

7 @ http://monsterkidclassichorrorforum.yuku.com/topic/1415#.Vp-Z5_krK70

Writer-director-actor Spencer Williams (Jr.) as the dopey-but-doggedly-determined Detective Nelson (ad-line: *"Can a Full-Grown Woman Truly Love a Midget?"*), early exploitation cinema impresario Esper continued re-exploiting the by-then-antiquated **INGAGI** (*"Explorers Find Living Girls Sacrificed To Gorilla Brutes!"*) to ever-diminishing returns on into the late '40s and early '50s (up until sometime in 1952, by all accounts). Lawsuits and threats of legal injunctions abounded over much of the course of **INGAGI**'s sensational run; but as any showman knows, there's no such thing as bad publicity, and we can only assume that all the negative press the film generated greatly increased its B.O. intake.

Rather than even pretending to have been filmed on the so-called Dark Continent, that phenomenally successful, allegedly $4-million-grossing film's bastard **SON**—who doesn't bear much of a family resemblance to his pops at all—stays much closer to home, however. And not only that, but its looming half-human/half-ape monster isn't played by a man in a gorilla suit; rather, it unfortunately more resembles a hippy black-and-white minstrel crossed with a 6½-foot-plus gollywog, as per a certain children's plush-toy that was banned for sale in the UK some years back due to its perceived negative racial connotations. As such, the creature is more pitiable than horrifying, especially in its earlier scenes before it undergoes a sudden "Mr. Hyde"-like metamorphosis into a vicious mangler of men. (Considering that artwork of a titanic snarling gorilla about a thousand times bigger than King Kong is seen looming over skyscrapers behind the opening titles, you might say that the film's actual monster comes as a bit of a letdown. One can only wonder at how many unsatisfied patrons might have demanded their money back!)

At the website Shock Till You Drop (*www. shocktillyoudrop.com*), in her article "10 Essential Black Horror Films"[8], Ashlee Blackwell waxed positive about the present film (even if she did mix up the writer/director/co-star's name with someone else's!):

"Screenwriter and actor Clarence [sic] *Williams had one goal in mind as a filmmaker: a film that elevated the image of African Americans during a time of great resistance by Hollywood in doing so. Not to be entirely entangled with the appalling 'documentary' that suggested African women breed with apes titled **INGAGI** from a decade earlier, **SON** was an exercise in centering Black characters, men and women, as scientists, lawyers, and interestingly, shows the vital*

8 Posted on February 23rd 2015 @ http://www.shocktilly-oudrop.com/news/374727-10-essential-black-horror-films/#/slide/1

communal structure to the Black community pre-1960s Civil Rights Movement. **SON** *could be read as a creature feature where Dr. Helen Jackson (Laura Bowman) keeps an ape/human hybrid in her home that eventually becomes brutish and homicidal. Heralded as the first Black horror/sci-fi film,* **SON OF INGAGI** *is a solid first in early cinema."* (That it is, and for that reason alone—as well as many other good ones besides—it absolutely *demands* our love and respect! Indeed, cries out for it, in fact. If a *Monster!* reader can't give it some love, who the hell else is gonna?)

The script was based on a story entitled "House of Horror", written by actor and occasional director Spencer Williams, Jr. (1893-1969), who later played the lattermost title character on CBS' *The Amos 'n Andy Show* (1951-53). Herein playing Detective Nelson, **SON OF INGAGI** was evidently the actor's sole foray into horror movies, although he did write, direct and/or appear in a number of other key early "Blaxploitation" entries, such as the present film's director Kahn's same-period western **TWO GUN MAN FROM HARLEM** (1938/40, USA), on which Williams only functioned in an acting capacity.

SON's likeable romantic leads Alfred Grant and Daisy Bufford whip up some convincing chemistry while playing a loving newlywed couple, Bob and Eleanor Lindsay, who at the outset of the film move into their new home, whereupon their friends show up and promptly throw a big shindig for them, apparently just to showcase a (pretty damn *good*!) vocal group called The Four Toppers (a.k.a. just The Toppers for short). For once we get some filler musical numbers (two in all) that really SWING! Dare I say *rock*, even. I mean, these cats totally *cook*! And, this *is* only 1940, don't forget: so rock'n'roll didn't even "officially" exist yet; yet here it is, raw and alive and comin' at ya, smooth as velvet. (Forget lip-synching to a recording, either. Their performance is captured live and in-camera, as-is). Many top musical acts of the time appeared in these films boasting an "all-colored cast". (Another one with some fine tuneage is the aforementioned ebony oater **TWO GUN MAN FROM HARLEM**, starring the long-lived "Herbert Jeffrey"/Herb Jeffries [1913-2014], an actor-singer who was at some time lead vocalist for Duke Ellington's band. In his ground-breaking book *From Sambo to Superspade* [Boston: Houghton Mifflin Co., 1975], author Daniel J. Leab wrote, "Certainly ghetto kids could look up to Herb Jeffries... just as their white counterparts admired Gene Autry." As with this issue's **KING OF THE ZOMBIES** [1941], **TGMFH** also features a memorable guest star turn from the mighty Mantan Moreland.)

Next door to our freshly-married hero and heroine at #1313 (*YIKES! Double thirteens!* Unlucky or what) resides frumpy, grumpy Dr. Helen Jackson (Laura Bowman), an elderly widow—and former missionary in Africa—with a major stash of life's savings (rumors of her fabled wealth prompt one of the film's wittiest lines, "They tell me that ol' lady's got enough money to burn-up a wet mule!"). The inclusion of a bona fide *female* scientist—a real rare bird indeed in old-age melodramas, even those of the predominantly white persuasion—is a surprising piece of liberal foresightedness for such a vintage bit of fluff as this, especially so since the character is not only a woman, but also black. This grouchily surly and seemingly antisocial doctress is befriended by the new bride ("I heard it was you paid the mortgage on the colored children's home…"). Beneath her gruff, tactlessly blunt exterior hides a heart of gold, however, as we subsequently realize.

A bit later into the narrative, intent on sleazing himself an exorbitant half-share of her $20,000 life's savings (in pure gold), which she brought back with her from Africa, the doc's no-good crooked IRS G-man brother Zeno (Arthur Ray) shows up at her house making demands…and threats. To solve this problem, Dr. Jackson bangs on a gong with the fancy Singaporean gong-striker she keeps handy, and—lo and behold—from behind a secret panel emerges N'Gina—a towering, hirsute apeman! (Doctor: "Don't look now, but there's a great big man right behind you!" – G-man: "*Hahaha!* Listen, Helen, that gag's as old as the hills. Why, they've even set it to *music!*" goes the hoary cliché.) However, the conniving brother soon beats a hasty retreat towards the nearest exit—diving headfirst straight out a window!—upon first sight of the unsightly N'Gina, whose looks are enough to turn a hog from its slop-trough. I mean, a plate of week-old chitterlings (i.e., "chitlins") looks lots more appealing than his butt-ugly mug does. Speaking of which, Zack Williams (1884-1958), the actor miming the part—and doing a pretty decent job of it, all things considered—wears monster makeup which mainly consists of what is essentially a shaggy "hair mask", with balaclava-like eye-nose-and mouth-holes cut out of it so as to leave all said facial features exposed. No offence intended to either actor, but for some strange reason, while watching Williams making various "animalistic" facial expressions, I couldn't help being reminded of the great Anthony Quinn in his 1957 portrayal of Quasimodo the hunchback, albeit with a lot more facial hair and minus the wonky eyeball!

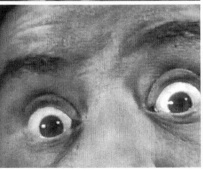

Top & Center: N'Gina, as seen both pre- and post- downing the serum that makes him go apeshit and transforms him into a homicidal brute. Can you tell which shot is "Before" and which is "After"? **Above:** Old Doc Jackson's eyes widen in terror as N'Gina approaches her with murder in mind

(See frame grabs nearby and decide for yourself if there's any resemblance.)

In her spare time, ol' Doc Jackson betters the course of Science, whipping together some Wonderful Discovery Vastly Beneficial To All Mankind without bothering to fill in the audience as to what it's even vaguely all about (we never

Top: This US one-sheet poster (art unsigned) intentionally kept its hairy monster's appearance vague in hopes it would bring to mind **INGAGI**'s gorilla and thus gull potential punters into believing it was a legit sequel to the 1930 roadshow hit. **Above:** N'Gina doesn't think that artist's impression looks anything like him!

do get a clue as to what use her serum was originally intended to be put. Not for turning [half-]men into monsters, surely?). "*I've got it!*" she triumphantly proclaims to N'Gina while they are alone together in her lab. "The greatest discovery in medicine since Louis Pasteur!" (Although perhaps Marie Curie might have been a more apt example to cite?) "...This is it. If it does what I think it will, I've done more for humanity than anyone else on Earth!" (like

I said, her great cause remains a mystery to us. Because the exceedingly battered and choppy print I saw was missing some scenes, perhaps a key expository one got lost somewhere along the line). Shortly thereafter, N'Gina foolishly—he is just a big dumb galoot, after all—drinks some of the doctor's latest wonder elixir, only to quickly be rendered a growling fury by the untested drug's instant adverse side-effect, attacking the recoiling she-scientist (of which, more below). Following the doc's untimely demise, her will stipulates that her newlywed neighbors shall be recipients of the late lady's estate, house inclusive. Complications shortly arise for the will's innocent beneficiaries, however, when John Q. Law in the form of blockhead flatfoot Nelson accuses new hubby Bob of murdering the late lady doctor in order that he and his wife could get their hands on her fortune early (not that they even knew they had been named as heirs to her estate; but how to convince pigheaded investigator Nelson of that?!). The gratefully bequeathed if bereaved couple gladly relocate, unaware of the secretly lurking cohabitant with "whom" (with *what?*) they are sharing the late Dr. Jackson's former abode. A short time after moving into their much more spacious (if gloomier and creepier) inherited new home, Daisy finds that somebody or other has been pilfering raw meat from the icebox and gobbling it all up ("...bones an' all!").

Leading man Alfred Grant possesses the look, presence and amiably affable acting style of a young Lon Chaney, Jr., except of course, he's black. Indeed, due to the high-contrast, overexposed state of the print I watched (an ancient '80s VHS tape from Sinister Cinema, which I ordered back in about 1988), it was difficult to really determine skin-tone much of the time, not that it matters. Though the cast here is 100% African-American (or perhaps mulatto?), Dr. Jackson especially appears Caucasian, although the actor playing her brother is clearly black. Prior to her demise, the doc keeps her (quote) "dumb friend" N'Gina in a barred (locked?) cell down in her basement, but periodically allows him upstairs to range freely about the house, considering him harmless. Only a total heartless bastard wouldn't be moved and touched by such intimate scenes of human interaction as the doctor and her in-house man-monster share! (I was rather reminded here of the touchingly affectionate mother/monster relationship between Anne Gwynne and Gil Perkins as the former and latter in Jacques R. Marquette's **TEENAGE MONSTER** [1957, USA; see *Monster!* #5, p.37].) Doc Jackson scolds N'Gina like an overgrown child for playing with knives ("*Bad boy!*") but fusses over him like a doting mother when he accidentally cuts his XL finger with one, slapping his other hand away lightly when he tries to mess with the dressing she puts on his wound (he subsequently pulls the bandage off and licks the blood from his hand afterwards, an action which might well be interpreted as a bit of ominous foreshadowing, considering the bloodthirsty monster he shortly becomes). Upon sipping some of his benefactress' supposedly beneficial formula without her knowledge while her back is turned, N'Gina's transformation into a ferocious beast occurs virtually instantaneously, although his already beastly physical appearance remains unchanged (he just starts grunting more and growling a lot louder to illustrate the change in him; oh yeah, and his face takes on a much fiercer expression to match his new foul disposition, too). Having started with just a sip, he then thirstily chugs back the entire test-tube full, then goes on a destructive rampage around the house prior to figuratively biting the hand that feeds him by literally murdering his matronly maternal substitute (albeit firmly off-screen). As the now-loco N'Gina advances into the camera—representing the doctor's POV—for a face-filling close-up, we cut to a second even more emphatic close-up of her terrified, wide-staring eyes, then still another emphatic close-up of an ink bottle toppling over during the scuffle and its dark contents spilling out; rather heavy-handedly if stylishly symbolizing "horrendous" violence occurring just out-of-frame during this scene. Because the film was (natch) shot in B&W, the spilled ink appears black, just as blood would, and this is what it registers as, such is the obviousness of the editor's juxtaposition. The effects of the serum evidently being permanent, N'Gina later goes on to throttle one of the couple's house guests, Dr. Jackson's lawyer Bradshaw (Earle Morris), who is acting as the executor of her estate. While the results of the monster's violence are never shown and gruesomeness is implied only after-the-fact in the dialogue (e.g., "...his neck was broken and two ribs caved in, and his back twisted [...] both arms was busted"), after being riddled with bullets N'Gina himself is clearly shown bleeding in several scenes; something you wouldn't ordinarily see in a mainstream Hollywood horror of the time. Presumably it was permissible to show his suffering more graphically than that of his victims for the simple reason that he was "just" the monster, after all, so it didn't matter (even if he did become more of one through no fault of his own simply for being too dumb to know any better). Sadly (☹), poor N'Gina winds up locked in his cage and goes up in smoke along with the house of horrors in the final reel; which isn't exactly a demise on the same grand scale as Kong's was, but we can't help feeling bad for the poor bastard anyway.

Most of the performances are highly enjoyable and naturalistic, with few discernible Mantan Moreland or Willie Best mannerisms in evidence (that latter actor was early in his career saddled with the consummately offensive stage-name "Sleep'N'Eat", FFS!); after all, the actors were playing to their own community in this one, so all the demeaning honky stereotypes needn't apply here. Spencer Williams as Nelson, the obligatory big/fat dumb detective on the case is an amusing standout; though he does occasionally rely rather too heavily on the bug-eyed "Feets, don't fail me now!" routine. Much screen-time is consumed having players wander about in the dark. This, added to the less-than-pristine nature of the print I am reviewing, causes small lapses in the intelligibility of certain visuals, whose cause is far from enhanced by the absolute absence of any incidental music. And **SON** sure crams a whole lot of plot complexities into its not-much-more-than-an-hour duration! However, there is a winning simplicity and sincerity to its execution, and a definite strand of humanism running throughout the story that makes it compelling.

Offering some clumsy comedic set-pieces (mainly at the big cop's expense), its share of substandard dialogue, and a sufficient quotient of schlocky apeman murders to nurture the film's quite brief duration, **SON OF INGAGI** illustrates an extremely dated, almost stage-bound method of moviemaking which looks a good ten years outdated even for the time at which it was made. Ultimately it is basically a black copycat of tried-and-true white formulae—even if the film is set in a then-impossible Never-Never Land in which even top-ranked social/authority figures are all black. However, some impression (no matter how tenuous) is conveyed of a vital subculture eager to express itself and break free of societal constrictions. And, more importantly, *do things its own way*. For these reasons it should be considered an "important" rung down the ladder of Blaxploitation's fitful evolution. As to whether or not it's a *good* film, despite what a number of other appraisals of it may have stressed over the years, is beside the point. It is what it is, and that fact in itself makes it historically important.

Interestingly enough, **SON**'s editor Dan Milner later went on to direct two low-end 'Fifties American monster movies, **THE PHANTOM FROM 10,000 LEAGUES** (1955 [see *Monster!* #18, p.24]) and **FROM HELL IT CAME** (1957 [see *Weng's Chop* #4.5, p.82]).

Fictional and non-fictional Cape Canaveral characters – **Top:** Sally (Linda Connell), Nadja (Katherine Victor), Tom (Scott Peters) and Hauron (Jason Johnson) on the cavern headquarters and laboratory set of **THE CAPE CANAVERAL MONSTERS** (1960/61); image and title card *[inset]*. **Bottom:** Dr. Wernher von Braun *[center]*, the NASA Director of the Marshall Space Flight Center, and President John F. Kennedy *[right]* at Cape Canaveral, Florida on November 16, 1963 (photo: NASA)

TUCKERED-OUT!

How the Creator of *Robot Monster* Brought the Talking Dead to NASA; Or, "If Your New Chin Needs a Little Trimming, I'll Fix It When I Get Back"

by Stephen R. Bissette

Among the most-forgotten—or, by those who remember it at all, the most-maligned—of all 1950s and early 1960s low-budget science-fiction movies remains Phil Tucker's bizarre, inventive, completely impoverished **THE CAPE CANAVERAL MONSTERS** *(1960, USA).*

It's another cheapjack movie I unapologetically love, and I recently reacquainted myself with it via the finest-looking transfer of the film I've ever seen, anywhere, on DVD (a boot from a fan-to-fan sale, alas, from Italy; it's never had an official home video release to my knowledge anywhere at any time, and this fan DVD-R even sported some nifty extras including period newsreel footage of rocket launches from the late 1950s and early 1960s and a cover gallery of the Italian 1950s Milano-based SF digest imprint I Romanzi di Urania*). There's precious little information out there about* **THE CAPE CANAVERAL MONSTERS**. *I've never found a single still or pressbook in all my years of collecting. To my mind, it's one of the real delights of early 1960s low-budget SF cinema, and at just 69 minutes, it's a brisker experience than its more renowned peers.*

TCCM didn't enjoy much of a showing anywhere or anytime; imdb.com *lists no release date for the film, and veteran cinema historian and Forgotten Horrors genre specialist Michael H. Price recently noted, "even the tradepapers seem to have overlooked this one,"[1] further evidence of it never having blemished a commercial theater screen. I've searched for decades for any evidence to the contrary, and never turned up a thing. Nor have I found any syndicated TV science-fiction or horror film package promotional material for the film (I have a few publications, including 1960s and 1970s syndication catalogues for TV stations, and it's not in any known genre pre-pack I've ever found paper on). Nevertheless, according to Kevin Heffernan's exhaustive research on genre film distribution,* TCCM *was part of a quartet of titles peddled in 1964 as the "Chiller-Science Fiction Package" syndication package of feature films for broadcast.[2] It popped up on local TV movie programming from time to time, including the late-night Canadian showing I caught in the late 1960s. We know for a fact it was shown on Milwaukee, Wisconsin's WISN-TV Channel 12 Movies from Tomorrow quite early on (in 1964, co-billed with 1959's* **THE KILLER SHREWS***), and again on WISN-TV's Shock Theater in 1983 (hosted by "Tolouse NoNeck" a.k.a. Rick Felski). It's also reportedly streamed on occasion on Netflix (starting in 2010, but it's no longer there now), which might—should the film surface there again—be the best option for* Monster! *readers to steep themselves in this unique curio.*

In the meanwhile, the curious history of **THE CAPE CANAVERAL MONSTERS** *continues to fascinate me.*

How is it that this grim black-and-white curio had the director of **ROBOT MONSTER** *circumstantially rubbing elbows with the likes of Mel Welles, Jerry Warren, and (*gasp!*) Ismael Merchant?*

Read on...

---

1   *Forgotten Horrors Volume 8: The Resurrection of Edgar Allan Poe* (2015, Cremo Studios), p.116; quoted with permission.

2   Heffernan, *Ghouls, Gimmicks, and Gold: Horror Films and the American Movie Business, 1853-1968* (Duke University Press, 2004), p.229.

Mexican lobbycard—stylized from the Astor Pictures American ad art—for Phil Tucker's infamous **ROBOT MONSTER** (1953)

Tucker was infamous in my own childhood and young adult years for his having directed the venerable 3D opus **ROBOT MONSTER** (1953), which was a staple late-night TV broadcast favorite for my generation. I'll never forget the write-up in the *Castle of Frankenstein TV Movie Guide* for **ROBOT MONSTER**, which (along with their write-ups of **PLAN 9 FROM OUTER SPACE, ORGY OF THE DEAD** [*M!* #19, p.21] and **TEENAGE MONSTER** [*M!* #5, p.37]) offered the first truly articulate codification of an aesthetic reaction to cinematic atrocities as being, in-and-of-themselves, alternate reality cinematic experiences of some interest and value.

Alas, less than a decade later, the Brothers Medved turned that into a cottage industry of sorts that continues into the 21st Century, launched with the book *The Fifty Worst Films of All Time (And How They Got That Way)* (1978) by Harry Medved, Randy Dreyfuss, and Michael Medved, and Harry and Michael's follow-ups *The Golden Turkey Awards* (1980) and *Son of Golden Turkey Awards* (1986). Ed Wood was vilified and lionized therein, as was Phil Tucker—but I still find much to honestly savor and enjoy in Phil Tucker's films, primary among them **THE CAPE CANAVERAL MONSTERS.**

These movies are easy to mock, but it must be reasserted that unlike, say, hucksters like Jerry Warren, Tucker was honestly doing the best he could with what resources he had. The gore quotient in **TCCM** was also unusual for mid-1960s TV broadcast—the damaged human bodies the aliens possess were ripped, torn, and bloodied in ways only TV broadcasts of the uncut **I WAS A TEENAGE FRANKENSTEIN** (1957) or **THE BRAIN THAT WOULDN'T DIE** (1959/62, both USA) shared in terms of such early black-and-white syndication broadcasts of horror movies—but what was even more unusual was the fact that the characters and dialogue really harped over the corporal damage the walking/talking possessed deadly duo suffered. Don't take my word for it, though.

Michael H. Price also offered his own anecdotal account of this, recalling how **TCCM** *"caused a sensation among monster-crazed schoolkids on account of its comparative wealth of bloody mayhem in the midst of an insipid and sanitized pop-cultural landscape"* in 1960s rural Texas where Price grew up. *"... 'Can they even get away with showing that stuff on teevee?' demanded one junior high-school chum. Well, yes, and of course 'they' could, whoever 'they' are, as long as 'they' kept such affronts away from the prime-time* *family-viewing hour. Most localized broadcasting stations presented the late-night spookers on autopilot, in any case, with commercial spots spliced into a 16-millimeter movie print at 15-minute intervals: Standard Operating Procedure—trip the projector-switch and leave the booth unattended."*[3]

TCCM also stands with a handful of other 1950s and early 1960s **NIGHT OF THE LIVING DEAD** predecessors that are made all the more interesting today in the context of what George Romero, John Russo, and their Image Ten partners accomplished in 1968. In magazines like *Films and Filming* (where the correlations between **THE BIRDS** and NOTLD were first articulated in print) and *Castle of Frankenstein* (where Calvin T. Beck cited a few of the following films as **NOTLD** predecessors), the first published advocacy of Romero and Image Ten's horrific independent horror film acknowledged a number of obvious precursors. These initially-cited influences were Alfred Hitchcock/Evan Hunter's **THE BIRDS** (1962) and Ubaldo Ragona's and Sidney Salkow's **THE LAST MAN ON EARTH** (*L'ultimo uomo della Terra*, 1964, Italy/USA; adapting the source novel Romero always cites, Richard Matheson's *I Am Legend* [see *M!* #13, pp.64-80]), while the more genre-savvy Beck in his lengthy *CoF* article added Ed Wood's now-immortal **PLAN 9 FROM OUTER SPACE** (1959), Edward L. Cahn's far-less-entertaining **INVISIBLE INVADERS** (1959), and Herk Harvey's truly uncanny, superior-in-every-way **CARNIVAL OF SOULS** (1962, all USA) to the list. Personally, I'd count Ray Kellogg's **THE KILLER SHREWS** (1959) as a primary thematic, pacing, and narrative template for **NIGHT OF THE LIVING DEAD**, but I'd also add Tucker's **THE CAPE CANAVERAL MONSTERS** and *The Outer Limits* episode "Corpus Earthling" (November 18, 1963) as essential "walking dead" predecessors to Romero's and Russo's revolutionary classic, if only in terms of atmosphere, imagery, and iconography. Tucker embraced **PLAN 9** and **INVISIBLE INVADERS** turf here: alien beings reanimating dead host bodies was a ghoulish variation on "alien possession" concepts introduced and popularized by Guy de Maupassant's "*Le Horla*" / "The Horla"

(1887), Shloyme Zanvl Rappoport a.k.a. Sholom Ansky's play *Der Dibuk / The Dybbuk* (1913-16), and then-more contemporary SF revamps of Robert Heinlein's *The Puppet Masters* (1951) and Jack Finney's *The Body Snatchers* (1955).

That duly noted, I don't want to overstate or lend any false pop-cultural caché to **THE CAPE CANAVERAL MONSTERS**. There's quite enough to love on its own modest, completely mongrel terms.

For openers, say what you will about Tucker's poverty of means; "CCM Productions" did afford three songs for the film via "special arrangement" with Lute Records, and relied upon cut-price but competent enough optical effects via Modern Film Effects to bring its "light beings" to the screen. With more efficiency than many of his peers, Tucker made great use of some pretty spectacular missile launch, misfire, and crash footage in **TCCM**. This footage lent the film what little spectacle it offers, but given the plethora of military stock footage padding many SF films in the 1950s (Nathan Juran's **THE DEADLY MANTIS** [1957, USA] was comprised of a startling quantity of such stock footage, for instance), I think it fair to credit Tucker for his effective use of what he had access to here. Newspapers occasionally featured blurry telephotos of NASA rocket test launches; by comparison, the test launch footage Tucker

Archival Cape Canaveral photo of the December 6, 1957 botched launch of the Vanguard TV-3; **CAPE CANAVERAL MONSTERS** made effective use of similar NASA misfire footage

3 Michael H. Price, *Ibid.*, pp.116-117. If memory serves, I caught **THE CAPE CANAVERAL MONSTERS** on CBC-TV Channel 6's Monday midnight late-night movie slot— listed in our local *TV Guide* as *Science-Fiction Theater*, though the broadcasts themselves never sported that title, but were always genre fare (SF, horror, fantasy)— and were shown uncut (even the American-International Pictures North American version of Mario Bava's **BLACK SUNDAY** [*La maschera del demonio*, 1960], was shown with all the gore AIP which had allowed for stateside release) and uninterrupted by commercials.

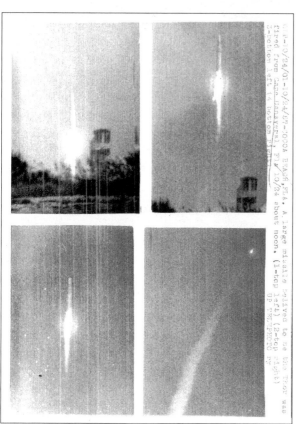

These aren't a result of shoddy scanning or poor printing! These are razor-sharp scans from vintage United Press "Telephotos" (i.e., photographs transmitted electronically, via a primitive, imperfect proto-FAX technology) which were by their very nature blurred and artifact-riddled. This is how my generation "saw" most of the Cape Canaveral launches, via newspaper-published telephotos and/or via "rabbit ears"-captured shaky video footage on the TV news; the official 16mm launch footage incorporated into films like **THE CAPE CA-NAVERAL MONSTERS** afforded us our best-ever look at such rocket tests. **Left:** The sequential four telephotos of the October 24, 1957 Cape Canaveral launch of "a large missile believed to be the Thor" (quoting the UP caption)

The UP telephoto caption read, "The Vanguard exploded on its launching pad in a huge ball of smoke and flame shortly before noon 12/6/57." (Images from the SpiderBaby Archives collection.) For more on the vintage transmission (and rescue) of space-race images, see *http://www.wired.com/2014/04/lost-lunar-photos-recovered-by-great-feats-of-hackerdom-developed-at-a-mcdonalds/*

utilized was remarkably crisp and clear. Tucker also made extensive use of familiar movie and TV western and genre film California landscapes, including—*yes!*—Bronson Caves, Griffith Park, Los Angeles, California.

Oh, Jesus wept.

The movie opens, *sans* titles, with two beads of blinding white light surging out of a pitch-black screen at the viewer. These blobs of light are the film's nominal "monsters", energy-beings from another (unnamed) planet.[4]

However rudimentary the filmmaking skills and budgetary means of Tucker, his grasp and ability to cobble together a movie was by this time sufficient shorthand for all that follows: the twin "balls" of light initially swell toward the viewer as the pulsing electronic sound effect grows louder, then retreats from the viewer as the sound diminishes. As the black background fades almost imperceptibly to a daylight shot of a ledge jutting up from a sandy beach, the two lights settle "into" niches in that rock as the surf rolls in.

A flat, affectless woman's voice, slightly distorted, is heard over this image of the lights pulsing on the rocks. "I told you we would find suitable bodies here, Hauron," she says, and Tucker's camera tracks screen left to follow tracks in the sand, leading us to a human couple on the beach. The light-beings spy on the couple: the woman runs back onto the beach from swimming, while the bored-looking man lackadaisically reads a book while halfheartedly sunbathing (wearing sunglasses and smoking a pipe). He hands her a white towel before methodically pulling on his white coveralls; she does the same after drying off, and they prepare to depart together. Tucker cuts away one time to the light-beings on the ledge as they vanish.

The two pulsing light-beings hitch a ride on the back bumper of the couple's car as they drive away from the beach. As they drive inland, the

Top: The two alien "light-beings" plunge toward the windshield of the car in the opening sequence, causing a fatal accident; a sequence much like this appeared in the Steven Spielberg/Robert Clouse TV feature **SOMETHING EVIL** (January 21, 1972).
Above: Now possessing the mutilated bodies of the driver and passenger, the "light-beings" swing into action as Nadja (Katherine Victor) reaches into the backseat to recover the now-reanimated driver's severed arm; the movie's first crude splash of *Grand Guignol*esque grue

---

lights vanish again, only to suddenly reappear right before the faces of the couple, prompting a fatal accident.[5] We see the bodies in the wreckage, clothing and faces streaming with blood, a lone blood-dripping arm hanging out of the back window (clearly belonging to a *third* performer hunkered down out-of-camera-view in the back seat, dangling his arm out the open back window!).

At this point, the still enigmatic voiceovers from "Earth Expedition #2", the male Hauron (vet TV actor Jason Johnson) and female Nadja (the marvelous Katherine Victor, best-known for her Jerry Warren outings), take over. The light beings possess the bloodied bodies of the couple, newly mobile as they make their way out of the passenger

---

4 Superficially similar to the "light-ball" extraterrestrial spy device in Curt Siodmak/George Worthing Yates/Bernard Gordon/Raymond T. Marcus/Fred F. Sears/Ray Harryhausen's **EARTH VS. THE FLYING SAUCERS** (1956, USA), Tucker's "alien light-beings" handily anticipate the fleetingly-glimpsed "light-beings" of Mario Bava and Ib Melchoir's **PLANET OF THE VAMPIRES** (*Terrore nello spazio*, 1965, Italy/Spain; light-beings which likewise possessed and reanimated the recently dead), Harry Essex's **THE CREMATORS** (1972), Bill Rebane's **INVASION FROM INNER EARTH** (a.k.a. **THEY** a.k.a. **HELL FIRE**, 1974, both USA), and many others. When budgets are low, nothing says "intangible alien being" like a flashlight beam or superimposed amorphous blob of light!

5 This sequence, crudely-executed as it was and is, anticipates a number of later supernatural thrillers in which inexplicable lights suddenly appear before drivers and cause fatal accidents, as in Steven Spielberg's US TV feature **SOMETHING EVIL** (January 21, 1972).

Philip Scheer (a.k.a. "Phil Schere")'s grue-some-for-1959 makeup effects for **THE CAPE CANAVERAL MONSTERS. Top to Bottom:** The MP carries Hauron's severed arm (torn from the latter's body by a guard dog) into the Mission Control lab, the bloody stump prominently displayed; the reanimated dead Nadja (Katherine Victor) badgers Hauron (Jason Johnson) about losing his arm— *again*; close-up of Katherine Victor's facial scar makeup, which she had to handle herself late in the filming after the lack of funds prompted Scheer to leave the production

view of the NASA control room. The militaristic music grows more urgent, and the white letters "CAPE CANAVERAL" appear on the screen in classic typewriter font; above and below, the smeared finger-painted words "THE" and "MONSTERS" appear, swell into place and joining the type-font titular location, then the title and credits proper unreel.

Within minutes of screen time, Hauron loses his freshly-transplanted arm *again* to a military police guard dog, and the guard carries the severed limb back to Mission Control (cue close-up of the severed, blood-dripping limb, and a tracking shot down the length of the limb to focus on the blood pooling on the floor). Thereafter, Nadja and Hauron become a bloodied, scarred, bickering couple entombed in their subterranean cavernous spaceship, the black heart of Tucker's invasion.

As in **ROBOT MONSTER** and Charles B. Griffith/Mark Hanna/Roger Corman's **NOT OF THIS EARTH** (1957, USA), the centerpiece of the invasion headquarters is a television monitor accessing "Leader" back wherever-the-hell-the-light-beings-came-from, with whom Hauron and Nadja banter as their sorry spearhead expedition fizzles. The reanimated dead couple putter and putz about with securing Earth specimens for study between successful attacks on Cape Canaveral missile launches. *Ro-Man, move over!*

Back at Mission Control, Dr. von Hoften (Billy Greene, wielding a risible German accent) puzzle over the mysterious and costly missile crashes, commanding a small team of scientists, including student Tom (Scott Peters) and von Hoften's niece Sally (Linda Connell, daughter of the film's cinematographer Merle Connell, in her only known screen role). With her uncle frowning on even minor attempts at fraternizing among the team—particularly from Tom towards von Hoften's own niece—Sally nonetheless contrives a night out in the convertible with fellow team scientist Bob (Gary Travis) and Bob's non-scientific date Shirley (Thelaine Williams).

While lazing about in a makeshift Lover's Lane with their transistor and car radios providing appropriately lovelorn pop music, Tom and Sally wander the nearby very-non-Floridian landscape trying to find the source of the annoying static (via their transistor radio picking up interference from Hauron's and Nadja's transmissions).

side of the car. After Nadja rescues the severed arm of Hauron's dead host body from the back seat, they hustle from the scene of the accident, urging each other to "Hurry! Hurry!"

Cut to: the first effectively edited dose of NASA stock footage, culminating in our first interior

Immediate cut to: *Interior* of Hauron's and Nadja's dark tech-grotto, where the alien "Leader" berates the deadbeat duo:

Leader: We need more Earthlings for our experiments, especially females.

Nadja: We will see to it, Leader. We have to make another capture anyhow—to repair Hauron's arm.

Leader: You must be more careful with the electroconvulsive shock and the freezing. The last ones you sent were dead when they arrived. It makes study extremely difficult.

Nadja: I will see to it.

They'd damn well better...!

———————

Tucker didn't have much false respect for his invaders—less, clearly, than he'd even afforded the diving-helmet-domed Ro-Man of **ROBOT MONSTER**, though it must be noted that despite the superficial story similarities to Wyott Ordung's screenplay for **RM**, Tucker made *this* invading couple unique. These deadpan, dour characterizations of alien interlopers make Tucker's SF films singularly endearing. Where Ro-Man puzzled over his place in the universe with pitch-perfect Catholic agonies ("I cannot—yet I *must*. How do you calculate *that*? At what point on the graph do "must" and "cannot" meet? Yet I must—*but I cannot!*"), Hauron and Nadja openly despise one another and barely pretend to get along, except when "Leader" is on the intergalactic shortwave. Their dual mission of downing any and all rocket launches and transporting human specimens to their home planet is somehow central to a pending largescale invasion (as Hauron later explains to the captive Tom).

Look, I'll just come right out and say it, since nobody else has ever has done so: Hauron and Nadja are the greatest zombie couple in all of 1950s and 1960s cinema, and we'd not see or hear their like again for decades.

For this alone, the movie is an unsung national treasure. This is why I love **THE CAPE CANAVERAL MONSTERS**: the constant bitchfest between alien-possessed-rotty-bodies Hauron and Nadja. This is priceless stuff, and unlike any previous zombie or space-zombie movie ever.

Hauron takes a lot of verbal abuse from Nadja, who just *loves* to rub it in about him losing that fucking arm. Nadja rubs Hauron's nose in that shit not once, but *twice*.

One of the two Ro-Man and "Great Guidance" helmets visible in Phil Tucker's **ROBOT MONSTER** (1953), devised by Al Zimbalist and Henry West for George Barrows to wear atop Barrows' own gorilla suit; compare this shot with the image on page 67

Hauron: We wait till after the launching to find more Earthlings. I can get by with one arm till then.

Nadja: Don't you owe it to the Council to use all your facilities for your work?

Hauron: Every missile from Cape Canaveral has either failed or was let go to avoid undue suspicion. Could you have done any better?

Nadja: Well I was just—

Hauron: I have to get this power pack get fixed-up right! Now, don't bother me again! Is that clear?

Nadja: Yes. Perfectly clear.

But there's more to this zombie couple than just the banter and bickering, and that, too, sets **TCCM** apart from its creepy, creaky kith and kin.

After Hauron uses a bazooka-like weapon to disrupt and crash another missile test launch, he immediately struts his stuff in front of a sneering Nadja:

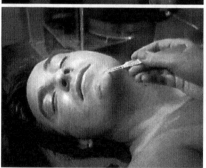

Le Menton Sans Visage: Kidnapped by the alien duo, Bob (Gary Travis) dies after his arm is surgically removed for transplant to replace Hauron's severed extremity—but Hauron also covets and claims Bob's *chin* to customize his scarred visage!

Hauron: I didn't do badly for a one-armed man, did I?

Nadja: Do we start looking for some specimens to send back now?

Hauron: No, I think not. Night seems like a better time. For now, we need some rest.

The latter line is delivered as Hauron suggestively strokes Nadja's torn-flesh-putty-ravaged cheek and scarred face.

What kind of "rest" do they "need", these two? Were these possessed corpses doing more than just "sleeping" together?

I was about eleven when I first saw this movie on TV, and even then, I shuddered and wondered...

While Tom and Sally stumble around in the dark trying to locate the source of the static fuzzing-out the music on Tom's transistor radio, wouldn't you know it: it's hapless Bob and Shirley who are ultimately abducted by the aliens. *Oh, unfair universe!*

This is, after all, a horror movie.

Tucker lets us know what the aliens have in store for Tom and Sally as Shirley is "prepared" and frozen for transmission to alien world.

Bob, though, suffers far *worse* indignities.

Hauron covets and surgically transplants Bob's healthy arm onto his shoulder stump. Bob succumbs to the post-surgical trauma, and after he dies, Hauron takes *his chin!*

I mean, *wow.*

His fucking <u>chin</u>.

Severing and reattached limbs is one thing.

Facial features—a chin—well, that's something else altogether. This proves almost as rich as Udo Kier's Baron von Frankenstein obsessing over his monster's *nasum* being sufficiently Serbian in Paul Morrissey's **FLESH FOR FRANKENSTEIN** (*Il mostro è in tavola...barone Frankenstein*, a.k.a. **ANDY WARHOL'S FRANKENSTEIN**, 1973, Ds: Paul Morrissey, Antonio Margheriti).

Nadja: He had a nice chin, except for that tiny scar.

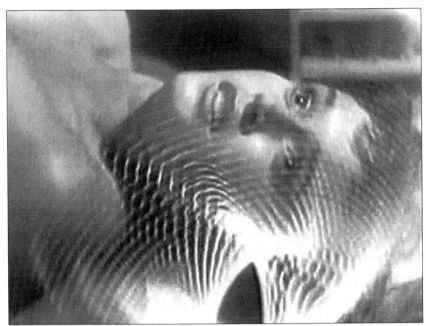

"She's unconscious now, but the Earthlings are strange": nude, unfortunate Shirley (Thelaine Williams) endures pseudo-psychedelic "electroconvulsive shock" prior to being frozen to send her bodily to the alien world Hauron and Nadja herald from

Hauron: Perhaps the more human I look, the more freely I could move around.

Nadja: His chin to replace yours... If your new chin needs a little trimming, I'll fix it when I get back.

C'mon, what's not to love?!

At this point, I must once again evoke the Pre-Code science-fiction and horror comics Eerie Publications was reprinting in the 1960s. When I first saw **TCCM**, damned if these bits with the aliens coveting limbs and a chin didn't make me think of (and dig out) my ragged, dog-eared stack of *Weird, Witches Tales*, and *Voodoo Tales* that very morning, and get my fingers and thumbs all black with smudgy-ink once again.

Typical of its era, genre, and low-budget niche, **TCCM** spins reels on presiding General Hollister (Chuck Howard) and the scientific team dismissing Tom's assertions before finally agreeing to investigate, with Tom escaping and being recaptured, light-being Hauron leaving his corpse host-body to take out a local law official (Matt Shaw), and Sally outwitting Hauron by giving him false information about the next launch, scuttling more sabotage and buying the time necessary

for General Hollister and the local deputy (Lyle Felisse) to attempt a rescue. They fail, but Hauron and Nadja decide it's time to hustle back home via their interstellar transport device—a distraction that allows Sally and Tom to escape, using the wee bit of radium on Tom's wristwatch against the imprisoning force-field. Hollister and company improvise the explosive demolition of Hauron and Nadja's cavern installation, and Sally departs with the law authorities—but a happy ending does *not* follow...

Though efficiently staged, none of this is particularly engaging. Hauron and Nadja, however, *are*. However maladroit Tucker's dramaturgy, his invading couple are caustic wonders. We even get a snippet of transcendental dialogue at one point from Hauron, when the imprisoned Bob tries to talk science with the admittedly-curious-about-this-particular-human-specimen Bob:

Hauron: Dreaming? Oh yes, sometimes when you humans are asleep, you see things that are not real. Hmph.

Shakespeare, it's not.

But once again, Tucker pauses to offer an odd interior meditative life for his "monsters", an

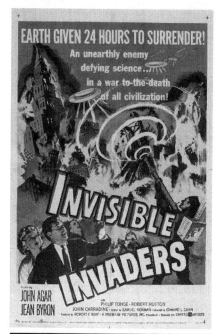

unusual grace note in an exploitation film made for pennies on the dollar.

I must add that when I first saw this loopy movie, I thought I'd dreamed the ending, which is even more abrupt and infuriating than the one Herschell Gordon Lewis grafted onto Bill Rebane's **MONSTER A GO-GO** (1966, USA).

SPOILER ALERT:

THE CAPE CANAVERAL MONSTERS boasted an early *WTF?!* bummer twist ending, implying within seconds that the invaders triumph via the cheapest imaginable trickery. I said no happy ending was in place:

As the last rescue car drives out of sight, with Bob and Sally safe and sound and the invaders apparently defeated, Tucker overdubs *the sound of a car accident*—you know the one, old-timers: *the* sound effect from the Standard Sound Effects Library 78 rpm record *Auto Crashes and Skids*, used in Jimmy Drake's 1956 45 record hit "Transfusion" and Jan and Dean's "Dead Man's Curve" and in every vintage road safety educational film and TV commercial about highway safety— followed by Sally's scream.[6] The screen goes black, and the light-blob abstractions of Hauron and Nadja flare into sight (as they did in the opening frames of the movie) till they swallow the screen, with the space-age sounds associated with them throughout roaring into our ears, then the credits roll. *The End.*

Again: What's not to love?

However sloppy the execution, this was pretty downbeat stuff for 1960, before such endings were *de rigueur*. If memory serves, Thomas Rogers (justifiably) included this in his *Famous Monsters of Filmland* #94 (November 1972) article listing all the shock twist-downbeat-endings of horror and SF films up to that point in time:

"The rocket-sabotaging **CAPE CANAVERAL MONSTERS** *(CCM, 1960) were balls of intelligent energy from another star system. Confident that their mission was a success, these aliens left Earth near the end of the film. As the rescued human protagonists drove away, secure in the belief that the invaders would not return, one car turned a bend and crashed. The screen went*

Top: Deceptively spectacular cataclysmic United Artists ad-art for the impoverished but influential **INVISIBLE INVADERS** (1959).
Center: Sally (Linda Connell) and Tom (Scott Peters) still exchange sweet-talk while imprisoned in the aliens' laboratory.
Bottom: Hauron (Jason Johnson) aims his phallic weapon toward another rocket test launch, downing the missile after liftoff ("I didn't do badly for a one-armed man, did I?")

6   You can hear this classic vintage car accident sound effect at *https://www.youtube.com/watch?v=FjpOboRcrNc*

blank, and the invasion of our planet began."[7]

That was far more than any other monster magazine of the era ever published about TCCM.

A lot of crap has been written about Phil Tucker over the years, with the smarmy passages in the Brothers Medveds' books treated as primary texts by most pundits—again, those being *The Fifty Worst Films of All Time (And How They Got That Way)* (1978) by Harry Medved, Randy Dreyfuss, and Michael Medved, and Harry and Michael's sequels *The Golden Turkey Awards* (1980) and *Son of Golden Turkey Awards* (1986). Tucker had lived long enough to have seen/read all but the last of the Medved tomes (Tucker died November 20, 1985, at 58 years of age), and had indulged being interviewed by the Medveds for *The Golden Turkey Awards*. He must have made peace with his past films by that time; whatever his limitations, Tucker had actually directed eight feature films and one short film between 1952 and 1955, surviving his initial reported despair and suicide attempt in December 1953[8] to continue working in the entertainment industry into the 1980s. Tucker's post-production supervisor and editing credits include feature films (Dino DeLaurentiis' monster movies **KING KONG** [1976], and **ORCA** [1977]; the *Get Smart* movie **THE NUDE BOMB** [1980]; **CHARLIE CHAN AND THE CURSE OF THE DRAGON QUEEN** [1980]; **OUT OF CONTROL** [1985], etc.), TV specials (for National Geographic's *Grizzly!* [1967] and *Amazon* [1968]) and movies (**WITH LOVE, SOPHIA** [1967]), and TV series like *The Next Step Beyond* (1978-79), *Wonder Woman* (1979

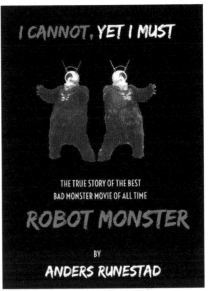

Two Ro-Men Are Better Than One: Cover art for Anders Runestad's astonishing new book *I Cannot, Yet I Must: The True Story of the Best Bad Monster Movie of All Time ROBOT MONSTER* (Radiosonde Books, 2016), absolutely essential reading for all *Monster!* devotees

---

episodes), as well as the live-action Saturday morning SF show *Jason of Star Command* (1979).

Thankfully, Anders Runestad's remarkable new book *I Cannot, Yet I Must: The True Story of the Best Bad Monster Movie of All Time ROBOT MONSTER* (self-published via Radiosonde Books, 2016) clears the record for all time on Phil Tucker. Runestad's *definitive* biographical tome on Tucker's life and film career offers a full context for and account of Tucker's **TCCM**, and all that followed for Tucker. Back in 2015, Runestad promised, *"There is indeed a chapter on* **THE CAPE CANAVERAL MONSTERS***! It's a pretty pivotal episode in Tucker's career too... it was a large, if relative, improvement on* **ROBOT MONSTER** *and it marked his last attempt to jump-start his movie career by making a low-budget movie. In the early '60s, he finally managed to get into the Hollywood mainstream doing editing and post-production work (often in documentaries), and making a living in show business is what he had wanted to do from early on."* [ellipses are in the original post being quoted].[9]

---

7 Thomas Rogers, "Shock-A-Bye Baby! A Fright List of American & British Horror Flicks With Shock & Surprise Endings. It's the Screaming End!," *Famous Monsters of Filmland* #94 (November 1972), p.10. Special thanks to David Beckham for confirming my memory, and for the timely access to this particular issue of *FM* when it was sorely needed.

8 "*Mirror* Halts Filmland Suicide," *The Mirror* (Los Angeles, CA), December 15, 1953 (pp.1, 3, 52), and "Movie Director's Death Try Balked: Letter Sent to Newspaper Results in His Being Found Unconscious in Room at Hotel," *Los Angeles Times*, December 16, 1953 (p.18). Anders Runested provides a full account of this stunt— no, I am not being flippant or cynical, this was a publicity ruse staged by Tucker and his pal Lenny Bruce (!)—in *I Cannot, Yet I Must: The True Story of the Best Bad Monster Movie of All Time ROBOT MONSTER* (Radiosonde Books, 2016), pp.313-323, 572. Tucker may have also completed a ninth film in the early 1950s, the never-released filmed-in-Alaska **SPACE JOCKEY** (see "Cast Hard at Work on Fairbanks' First Movie," *Fairbanks Daily News-Miner*, August 5, 1953); see http://www.imdb.com/name/nm0875973/board/nest/246864392?ref_=nm_bd_1 for a cleaned-up text from this article; Runestad covers **SPACE JOCKEY** extensively, too (see his book, pp.279-317).

9 For more information, see http://monsterkidclassichorrorforum.yuku.com/topic/60145/Making-of-ROBOT-MONSTER-Book-Coming-Soon-in-2015?page=1#. Vm3tphzDZIY and http://monsterkidclassichorrorforum.

In his chapter on **TCCM**, Runestad builds upon Tom Weaver's published interview with co-star Katherine Victor[10]—along with the Medveds' account of Tucker's post-**ROBOT MONSTER** career and Bill Warren's review of the film in his justly celebrated *Keep Watching the Skies!*, published interviews with Katherine Victor are the only previous print records of note on **TCCM**— to chronicle what led to the making of the feature, its production, and the fate of the completed film. Harry Medved provided Runestad with a transcript of the interview Tucker indulged for the Medveds, and Runestad also interviewed Tucker's son Phil Tucker, Jr. for his definitive book, but still must proffer speculative possible answers to the many riddles of **TCCM**'s creation and eventual release.[11]

Emerging from Tucker's enigmatic "lost" feature **PACHUCO** (1956?)—which may or may not have ended up actually being Tucker's **BROADWAY JUNGLE** (1955, USA), though Runestad effectively argues against that notion— Runestad builds his case around Tucker's possible, fleeting involvement and death of producer, distributor, and poverty-row mogul A.W. "Bill" Hackel, whose Supreme Pictures ground out Bob Steele and Johnny Mack Brown westerns in the 1930s. Hackel continued producing films for Monogram in the 1940s before retiring from the industry; Hackel died on October 21, 1959, and his death becomes a critical reference point in Runestad's teasing-out of the most likely scenario behind the launch of **THE CAPE CANAVERAL MONSTERS**. A quote from the Medved summary of the taped interview with Tucker provides Tucker's possibly-faulty memory of the circumstances behind the funding of the project, linked with Tucker's false suicide attempts:

"Mr. Tucker dismissed these suicide attempts as mere gimmicks in order to procure free room and board. Tucker became friends with the psychiatrists at the hospital, and they soon decided to help him out with his financial troubles. As a favor, four of the psychiatrists at the Veterans' Administration decided to put up the money for him to direct another film, which was entitled [THE] CAPE CANAVERAL MONSTERS... His film... however, was put in the vault for a year and was not released until 1961."[12]

Based upon Katherine Victor's account of the film's production to interviewer Tom Weaver, Runestad concludes that **TCCM** was most likely filmed in December 1959. In that interview, Victor recalled, "We shot the interiors at a small independent studio on Western Avenue in Hollywood. The cave scenes were shot in Bronson Canyon and the beach scenes at Malibu. I remember it was December and it was freezing!"[13] As for further details of its production, Runestad cites actor/author Barry Brown's interview with Katherine Victor, which revealed that Tucker had initially planned for a two-week shoot of a color film via the film's credited producer and editor Richard Greer "arranged for healthy financing through the investments of a group of doctors," but that eleventh-hour budget cuts slashed both the duration of the filming and relegated it to being a black-and-white feature, not color.[14] As Runestad notes, it "is certain the executive producer Lionel Dichter practiced medicine for decades and Harriet Dichter, silently appearing first after the credits as a scientist, was his wife."[15] As to **TCCM**'s eventual distribution limbo, Runestad offers interview evidence of Tucker having offered the film to Universal for possible distribution,[16] and tracked down April-July 1961

yuku.com/reply/1146679/Making-of-ROBOT-MON-STER-Book-Coming-Soon-in-2015#reply-1146679, where author Anders Runestad noted having a print proof copy in hand as of November 2015. We eagerly recommend *Monster!* readers buy their copy now that it's available! Highest recommendation; see *www.runestadwrites.com* and *http://www.amazon.com/Cannot-Yet-Must-Story-Monster/dp/0692576622/*

10 Tom Weaver, *Science Fiction Stars and Horror Heroes: Interviews with Actors, Directors, Producers and Writers of the 1940s-1960s* (McFarland, 1991)

11 Lest anyone attack my writing or *Monster!* publishing this article as merely piggy-backing on Anders Runestad's marvelous book, please note that I originally wrote and published (online, via my blog *Myrant*) the original draft of this essay back on February 1, 2013, long before Anders even announced his book project publicly. I hope it is also self-evident that I continue to try and add further insights and my own original research efforts to Runestad's, which handily and definitively outstrips his of anyone to come before him. Note that I have dedicated this article in part to Runestad, and do so with only the most honorable of intentions and most profound respect.

12 Harry Medved, "typed transcript of Phil Tucker interview," quoted by Runestad, *I Cannot, Yet I Must: The True Story of the Best Bad Monster Movie of All Time ROBOT MONSTER*, p.482.

13 Weaver interview with Victor, *Ibid.*, p.392.

14 Brown interview with Katherine Victor, in *Scream Queens: Heroines of the Horrors* by Calvin T. Beck (MacMillan, 1978), p.236. Beck, of course, was the editor/publisher of the newsstand monster magazine *Castle of Frankenstein*, and Barry Brown was an author, playwright and actor (**THE GREAT NORTHFILED MINNESOTA RAID** [1972], **BAD COMPANY** [1972], **DAISY MILLER** [1974], **PIRANHA** [1978]) and former contributor to *Films in Review*, *Castle of Frankenstein*, and Beck's books who sadly committed suicide on June 25, 1978 at the age of 27.

15 Runestad, *Ibid.*, p.492.

16 See Paul and Donna Parla, "The Batwoman from Cape Canaveral: An Interview with Katherine Victor," *Filmfax* #58 (October 1996), p.43. In her interview with the Parlas, Victor specifically cited a budget of "around $150,000."

Mexican ad art for Mel Welles' set-in-Mexico **CODE OF SILENCE** (1961), the final film actually released by Sterling World Distributors; note Roger Corman and Jerry Warren regular Bruno VeSota prominent in this lobby card.
Previous Page: George Barrows (as Ro-Man), George Nader, and Claudio Barrett in a posed publicity photo for **ROBOT MONSTER** (1953)

Variety articles involving the California Division of Labor Law Enforcement's prosecution of "Cape Canaveral Monsters Inc. and C.C.M. Prod. Inc." for non-payment of the film's primary cast members, "money... owed performers more than a year," and the fact that the defendants claimed that "Sterling World Distributors, handling pic, has not yet turned any cash for distribution to producers or Phil Tucker, prexy" (Runestad must be applauded for his intensive research efforts and results).[17]

What Runestad doesn't comment upon is how perfectly Sterling World Distributors Corp.'s fleeting track record fits the timeline, as does the distributor having evaporated from the marketplace in 1961, leaving Tucker and his partners stranded and dealing with the film's debts. But the association with Sterling World Distributors also places Tucker and **TCCM** among a most curious associative link with filmmakers like Ismael Merchant and Mel Welles, which is quite a stretch. Sterling World, whatever their initial ambitions, amassed an odd track record within a short two years, having theatrically distributed the English-dubbed version of Miguel Contreras Torres' 1958 Mexican western **THE LAST REBEL** (*El ultimo rebelde*) in 1961, plus **THE HALF PINT** and **GET OUTTA TOWN** (both 1960, USA), the Oscar-nominated Ismail Merchant-produced short film *The Creation of Woman* (1961, India/USA) and Mel Welles' **CODE OF SILENCE** (1961, USA). Despite the nominal prestige earned by

Sterling's release of Merchant's *The Creation of Woman* landing an Academy Award nomination, short films were hardly lucrative fare by 1961, as American theaters phased-out the programming of shorts (much less adventurous booking of a short film from India) other than cartoons. The more prestigious Janus Films picked up *The Creation of Woman* after Sterling's nominal release.[18] Exploitation was Sterling's bread-and-butter, as the surviving promotional materials from the films they did release proves. Import fare like Torres' aforementioned **THE LAST REBEL** was ballyhooed with taglines like *"His Naked Guns Blazed a Trail of Terror!"* and *"He Branded an Entire State with... REVENGE!"* while their Los Angeles-set-and-shot crime opus **GET OUTTA TOWN** featured burly, outsized Doug Wilson with fist raised, standing above a dwarfed cityscape: *"When Gangsters Killed His Kid Brother, Kelly Turned the City Upside Down!"* Mel Welles' **CODE OF SILENCE** was similarly a crime film, promoted with a striking graphic of a fist clenched around a chain (*"Hero... or Criminal? Caught Between the FBI and the Syndicate... He Waited for the Final Payoff!"*); it was theatrically released in Mexico (in February 1963, as **F.B.I. CONTRA EL CRIMEN**) and subsequently dumped into TV broadcast syndication as **KILLER'S CAGE** after Sterling's dissolution. One can only imagine what lurid taglines and eye-catching ad art Sterling might have mounted to promote **THE CAPE CANAVERAL MONSTERS**!

With Sterling defaulting on payments due Tucker and C.C.M. and no subsequent luck interesting Universal in handling **TCCM**, it's no surprise that genre historians like Bill Warren and Michael H. Price have never found trade publication notices for the movie. By all evidence, the film was dumped into television distribution within four years of its completion, making it highly unlikely that any theatrical promotional materials were *ever* created for the film, and I've never found any TV syndication promo materials for **TCCM**, either. As veteran collector and dealer of movie memorabilia Bruce Hershenson noted to me in a recent Facebook conversation, *"I have NEVER auctioned even a single still, lobby card or poster*

17 Runestad, *Ibid.*, pg. 493, citing and quoting *Variety*, April 5, 1961, p.56, and *Daily Variety*, July 3, 1961, p.3. The April 5 *Variety* article noted that **THE CAPE CANAVERAL MONSTERS** was "reportedly made at Telepix Studios in close to ten days."

18 *The Creation of Woman* can be screened online at https://www.youtube.com/watch?v=oCPNdRJiR6Q and is on DVD on Criterion's "The Merchant Ivory Collection" DVD of James Ivory's **THE HOUSEHOLDER** (1962; at http://www.amazon.com/Householder-Sword-Creation-Merchant-Collection/dp/B0001GH5SS/ref=sr_1_fkmr0_1?ie=UTF8&qid=1452447936&sr=8-1-fkmr0&keywords=The+Householder+Ismael+Merchant). The primary dancer onscreen in *The Creation of Woman* is Bhaskar Roy Chowdhury, a.k.a. Bhaskar, who later starred in David Durston's incredible rabid-hippies-vs.-rabid-construction-workers opus **I DRINK YOUR BLOOD** (1971, USA).

Bootleg DVD art—back cover/spine/front cover—lifting cover images and logos from two issues of the Italian SF digest magazine *I Romanzi di Urania* (inserting their own makeshift **THE CAPE CANAVERAL MONSTERS** title into the front cover graphic), a surprisingly effective evocation of the period flavor and imagery of the film (scanned from the SpiderBaby Archives)

from it. The paper from it is beyond rare! If it had a theatrical release in even one theater, they surely had SOMETHING to advertise it. There are a very few movies where they only used homemade advertising at one or a few theaters that showed the film, but I have seen pressbooks on the absolute most obscure movies, so there is still a tiny bit of hope something COULD turn up one day... If it was never exhibited theatrically, then the odds are great there was no paper. But sometimes paper WAS created for a hoped-for release, so there is a tiny chance something could turn up. But since I have auctioned entire collections of people who spent 30 to 40 years trying to get something from every horror/sci-fi movie, and NONE of them ever had anything, I would say the chances of finding something are statistically close to zero!"[19]

Such are the cruelties of the marketplace. In the end, Runestad's research revealed that *"copyright records assign it to CCM Productions, Inc. ("employer for hire") and Republic Pictures as of March 1, 1960... It is possible that March 1, 1960 simply refers to the copyright of the film, and there was a much longer period of selling the film before Republic picked it up and presumably*

got some television money for it... That *THE CAPE CANAVERAL MONSTERS was dumped on television is explained by the 1959 sale of Republic's library to National Telefilm Associates. As years went by, it went with the rest of Republic's catalog to become the property of [Artisan] Entertainment and then Lionsgate."*

Runestad chalks up Republic's eventual acquisition with the associative links he discovered between Tucker, A.W. "Bill" Hackel, the foiled Tucker feature **PACHUCO**, and Republic:

"Hackel had deep roots in Republic... with the production of THE CAPE CANAVERAL MONSTERS beginning within two months of Hackel's death, there is an overwhelming circumstantial sense that it might have gone to Republic because of some connection to PACHUCO, perhaps as a last resort or even to settle an obligation. Without Hackel's involvement in PACHUCO, perhaps CANAVERAL would have gone to another distributor and played theatrically."[20]

As Runestad notes, whatever its detriments, **TCCM** was superior to many genre films of the

19 Hershenson, Sunday, January 10, 2016 Facebook conversation with Bissette; quoted with permission. Thank you, Bruce!

20 Runested, *Ibid.*, pp. 495-496. For more on the film, see Runestad's complete chapter, pp. 481-511.

MONSTERS ATTACK EARTH!

3D

ADVENTURES INTO THE FUTURE in New TRU-3 DIMENSION

ROBOT MONSTER

MOON LAUNCH MONSTERS EARTH ATTACK

GEORGE NADER
CLAUDIA BARRETT

The crazy-quilt Astor Pictures Corp. ad art for the original 3D release of **ROBOT MONSTER** (1953) shamelessly lifted promo images from Warner Bros.' contemporary **THE BEAST FROM 20,000 FATHOMS**, the cheapjack **TWO LOST WORLDS** (1951), and classic paleo art by Charles Knight; some historians argue the stylized skull-faced Ro-Man image was calculated to suggest a variant on **KING KONG** (1933), which RKO had just re-released in 1952 to smash-hit boxoffice earnings

period that somehow *did* secure theatrical releases. Runestad names **THE BRAIN THAT WOULDN'T DIE** (1959/62), **THE BEAST OF YUCCA FLATS** (1961), and **MONSTER A-GO GO** (1961/65), but I'd line up widely-released titles like Bruno VeSota's **INVASION OF THE STAR CREATURES** ([1962] co-featured by American-International Pictures with **THE BRAIN THAT WOULDN'T DIE**), Vic Savage's **THE CREEPING TERROR** (1964, all USA), or any one of Jerry Warren's abominations against Tucker's **THE CAPE CANAVERAL MONSTERS** any day to find Tucker's still seeming like a far more commercial venture. But the vagaries of the marketplace determine everything: **THE BRAIN THAT WOULDN'T DIE** malingered unreleased for three years until AIP picked it up as a co-feature for the woeful **INVASION OF THE STAR CREATURES** (which was, at least, quite candid about its calculated trash status, opening with the satiric bogus byline "R.I. Diculous Present"), and it's only because Herschell Gordon Lewis needed a co-feature for 1964's **MOONSHINE MOUNTAIN** that he picked up and finished Bill Rebane's uncompleted 1961 SF feature and released it as **MONSTER A-GO GO** in 1965. If only Sam Arkoff and James Nicholson at AIP had needed a co-feature; if only…

In all other matters relating to the movie, I humbly defer for the most part to Runestad (and hope that what I've written here still adds something to reconsideration of the film). However, Runestad's estimation of the movie itself seems lower than my own, summing it up as "not a great or even good film and on its own merits did not deserve much publicity, but it is Tucker's finest work as a director… it has a sophistication and smoothness absent in his earlier movies."[21] True enough, but it's the over-the-top characterization of the invaders that make **THE CAPE CANAVERAL MONSTERS** an essential experience to me.

Seen today, on its own meager terms, **TCCM** still benefits from what production muscle Tucker was able to mobilize. Once the electronic sound effects subside in the pre-credits sequence, Gene Kauer's musical score (credited to "Guenther" Kauer) propels the soundtrack and keeps things moving. The German composer had been scoring similarly impoverished fare from the get-go: **THE ASTOUNDING SHE-MONSTER** (1957), **MA BARKER'S KILLER BROOD** (1960),

21 Runestad, *Ibid.*, p.483-484.

and his uncredited score for **THE BEAST OF YUCCA FLATS** (1961, all USA) provides the context for his work on TCCM. Kauer continued to score low-budget far like the Johnny Cash-as-psychopath **FIVE MINUTES TO LIVE** (a.k.a. **DOOR-TO-DOOR MANIAC**, 1961/64), **MONSTROSITY** (a.k.a. **THE ATOMIC BRAIN**, 1963), **FORTRESS OF THE DEAD** (1965), **AGENT FOR H.A.R.M.** (1966, all USA), **WARKILL** (1968, USA/Philippines), **CLAWS** ([1977] credited as "Gene Kaver"), the *Faces of Death* series (1978-85+), **MONSTER** (a.k.a. **MONSTROID**, 1980, all USA), and **THE ONE ARMED EXECUTIONER** (1981, Philippines), along with work on *The Gumby Show* (1966) and soundtrack scores for family films like **BROTHER OF THE WIND** (1973), **THE ADVENTURES OF THE WILDERNESS FAMILY** (1975), **ACROSS THE GREAT DIVIDE** (1976), and **THE FURTHER ADVENTURES OF THE WILDERNESS FAMILY** (1978, all USA) balancing the karmic scales a bit.

Co-producer and editor Richard Greer had cut his teeth as assistant editor on Ronnie (**THE ASTOUNDING SHE-MONSTER**) Ashcroft's **GIRL WITH AN ITCH** ([1958] another feature which Kauer had scored), landing his first and only 1960s feature film producer-editor credits on TCCM before launching into his TV career as production coordinator and editor for episodes for *Mr. Ed* (1964-66), *The Addams Family* (1964-66), *The Beverly Hillbillies* (1967-69), *Petticoat Junction* (1967-69), and *Project U.F.O.* (1978-79, all USA). Greer also edited now-celebrated exploitation features like **CLASS OF '74** (1972), **BONNIE'S KIDS**, **THE CANDY SNATCHERS** and **DETROIT 9000** (all 1973, all USA), **WONDER WOMEN** (1973, USA/Philippines), **THE CENTERFOLD GIRLS** (1974), and **LINDA LOVELACE FOR PRESIDENT** (1975, both USA), among others.

The slapdash but grisly makeup effects were the work of Philip Scheer, credited here as "Phil Schere". Scheer deserves a *Monster!* gallery of his own; though he was a no-nonsense makeup expert who'd worked for early television (*The Life of Riley* [1949-1950]; the *Disneyland* episodes released theatrically as **DAVY CROCKETT AND THE RIVER PIRATES**, [1955/56], etc.) and lots of low-budget films, Scheer left an indelible creative mark on 1950s genre fare. While his rogue's gallery may not be as iconic as that of peers like Paul Blaisdell, Harry Thomas, or greats like Jack Pierce (latter of whom was laboring in similarly impoverished

productions after Universal unceremoniously "retired" him after World War II, this after three decades working for the studio and creating all its classic monsters to that point), Scheer had already been up-to-his-eyeballs in monster movie makeup, including **I WAS A TEENAGE WEREWOLF**, **BLOOD OF DRACULA** and **I WAS A TEENAGE FRANKENSTEIN** (all 1957), **ATTACK OF THE PUPPET PEOPLE** and **HOW TO MAKE A MONSTER** (both 1958), and **INVISIBLE INVADERS** (1959, all USA), cementing his as-yet-unacknowledged claim-to-fame as creator of one of the prototypes for the "look" codified by **NIGHT OF THE LIVING DEAD** (1968). In fact, Scheer's first screen credit was as hairstylist for **REVOLT OF THE ZOMBIES** (1936, USA)! According to Katherine Victor, Scheer was a casualty of the budget constraints in the final days of the filming, "and at that point she became her own makeup artist."[22]

Along with writer-director Phil Tucker, editor Greer, and makeup effects creator Scheer, there's some credentials attached to the cast members of interest to genre devotees. Nominal hero Scott Peters cut his acting teeth doing a lot of TV, along with roles in such theatrical features as **INVASION OF THE BODY SNATCHERS** (1956), **MOTORCYCLE GANG** and **THE AMAZING COLOSSAL MAN** (1957), **ATTACK OF THE PUPPET PEOPLE** and **HOT ROD GANG** (both 1958), **THE FBI STORY** ([1959] appearing, uncredited, as John Dillinger!), **PANIC IN YEAR ZERO!** (1962), **THE GIRL HUNTERS** (1963), and in David Bradley's astonishing **MADMEN OF MANDORAS** (a.k.a. **THEY SAVED HITLER'S BRAIN**, 1963/68, all USA). He's best-known to my generation, though, for having played Detective Valancia on *Get Christie Love!* (1974, USA).

Better yet is the fact that heroine Sally was played by stylishly short-haired ingénue Linda Connell, in her one and only screen role. As already noted, Linda was the daughter of W. Merle Connell, the vet cinematographer who shot **THE CAPE CANAVERAL MONSTERS** for Tucker. Connell was credited here as "Merle Connell", along with Tucker's earlier Lenny Bruce vehicle **DANCE HALL RACKET** (1953) and Tucker's documentary-exposés **TIJUANA AFTER MIDNITE**, **DREAM FOLLIES** and

---

22 Runestad, *Ibid.*, p.490, paraphrasing from Tom Weaver's interview with Victor in *Science Fiction Stars and Horror Heroes: Interviews with Actors, Directors, Producers and Writers of the 1940s-1960s*.

ROGUES

You'd think every monster-maker of the 1950s would have been properly celebrated by now, but no! Here's a *Monster!* Rogues Gallery for low-budget makeup magician Philip Scheer (a.k.a. "Phil Schere" in **THE CAPE CANAVERAL MONSTERS** credits), whose numerous 1940s-1960s movie and TV series makeup creations included some of the Fabulous Fifties' iconic creatures.

From Top Left to Bottom Right: 1. Michael Landon's breakthrough starring role relied upon Scheer's lycanthropy makeup for **I WAS A TEENAGE WEREWOLF** (1957). 2. Gosh, how did Scheer's makeup effects make the cast of Bert I. Gordon's **ATTACK OF THE PUPPET PEOPLE** (1958) so tiny?! 3. Looking very much like his **CAPE CANAVERAL MONSTER** creations, this alien-reanimated dead man was one of a plethora of Scheer makeups for

GALLERY

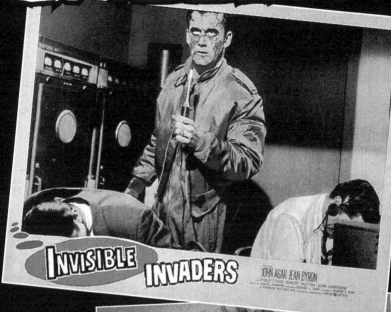

INVISIBLE INVADERS

JOHN AGAR · JEAN BYRON

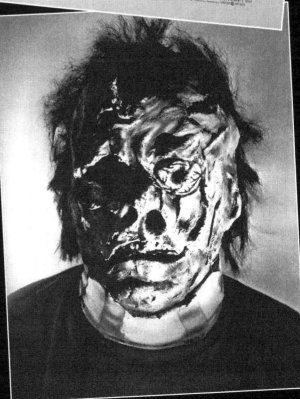

Edward L. Cahn's **INVISIBLE INVADERS** (1959). 4. Gary Conway (whose face did appear relatively undamaged towards the end of the film, and who a decade later was the nominal hero of Irwin Allen's TV series *Land of the Giants*) had his face "Scheered" away thus in **I WAS A TEENAGE FRANKENSTEIN** (1957). Note: See our back cover for Scheer's bizarre female vampire makeup design for Herman Cohen's **BLOOD OF DRACULA** (1957)

Katherine Victor *[center]* as Dr. Myra—whose foreign-funded scheme to turn the entire population of America into zombies was foiled by the surrounding cast members—in this shot from Jerry Warren's **TEENAGE ZOMBIES** (1960); that's **THE GIANT GILA MONSTER** and **THE REBEL SET**'s Don Sullivan about to slip Dr. Myra a mickey

BAGDAD AFTER MIDNITE (all 1954, USA), and **STRIPS AROUND THE WORLD** (1955, USA). *Pater* Connell was also the director of a string of almost iconic low-budget exploitation gems, including **A NIGHT AT THE FOLLIES** (1947), **HOMETOWN GIRL** and **TEST TUBE BABIES** (both 1948), **THE DEVIL'S SLEEP** and **TROUBLE AT MELODY MESA** (both 1949), **INTERNATIONAL BURLESQUE** (1950), **DING DONG** (1951), the beloved—well, to *some* of us! *[Me included ☺ – SF.]*—**ONE MILLION B.C.** stock-footage feast **UNTAMED WOMEN** (1952), **THE FLESH MERCHANT** (1956), and **NOT TONIGHT HENRY** (1960, all USA).

That's a lot of exploitation history behind the screen of such a low-budget SF film, making it all the more remarkable that **TCCM** remains so obscure even among connoisseurs of the bizarre. Still, others have tried to add to its allure in this department via misidentification of a supporting cast member, Lyle Felice (who appears as one of the local police swept-up in busting the alien invasion). Many continue to conflate Felice with a young Al Adamson—future director of exploitation films like **BLOOD OF GHASTLY**

HORROR ([1972] a reworking of Adamson's earlier **PSYCHO A-GO-GO** [1965], and **THE FIEND WITH THE ELECTRONIC BRAIN** [1966]), **BLOOD OF DRACULA'S CASTLE** and **SATAN'S SADISTS** (both 1969), **DRACULA VS. FRANKENSTEIN** (1971), **BRAIN OF BLOOD** (1972, all USA), etc.—claiming Adamson himself played the role under the screen name "Lyle Felice." Adamson's long-time production/distribution partner Sam Sherman put this to rest on his DVD commentaries for **BLOOD OF GHASTLY HORROR**, and Anders Runestad reasserts Sherman's clarification in his definitive biography of Phil Tucker: Sam says, "Al Adamson and Lyle Felice are not the same person."[23] 'Nuff said.

The crowning glory of **THE CAPE CANAVERAL MONSTERS** was and remains the venomous back-and-forth between ravaged zombie co-stars Jason Johnson and Katherine Victor. Johnson was in too many TV shows to list—oh, hell, here goes: *The Clock* (1950), *Gang Busters* (1951), *Robert Montgomery Presents*

23 Sam Sherman, commentary track for Troma Entertainment Inc.'s February 27, 2001 DVD release of **BLOOD OF GHASTLY HORROR**, with **PSYCHO A-GO-GO**. Also see Runestad, *Ibid.*, pp.493-494.

(1950 and '52), *Highway Patrol* (1956), *Sergeant Preston of the Yukon* (1955 and '56), *Science Fiction Theatre* ([1956] including, interestingly enough, "The Living Lights" episode), *Playhouse 90* (1956 and '57), *Circus Boy* (1957), *The Lone Ranger* (1957), *The Adventures of Superman* (1958), *Father Knows Best* (1958), *Studio 57* (1958), *The Adventures of Jim Bowie* (1956-58), *The Rifleman* (1959), *Laramie* (1959), *Zane Grey Theater* (1958-1960, all USA) and so on and so forth into the late 1970s. Johnson also had roles in big-screen outings like **INVASION OF THE SAUCER MEN** (1957), **I WANT TO LIVE!** (1958, both USA), and many more. Johnson was a true working actor and an omnipresent player for my generation's boob-tube habits.

Katherine Victor, though, was a more rarified player and cultivated taste, having been relegated primarily to the ill fortunes and ample screen-time that producer/director Jerry Warren padded-out running times with, both making and breaking Victor's career over the course of a little more than a decade.

She is splendid in **TCCM**, making the most of every nitpicking line (especially over that lost arm!) and positively seething from the screen when she gets the upper hand on the lowly Earth patsies. Tom Weaver (who should know!) notes that Katherine was born Katena Ktenavea "in the Hell's Kitchen district of Manhattan…grew up in Los Angeles and began her acting career on the stage and radio in the late '40s."

Victor made her film debut (as "Katina Vea") as one of mad scientist Jackie Coogan's "spider women" in the notorious Ron Ormond atrocity **MESA OF LOST WOMEN** (1952, USA), but I first saw her while struggling to stay awake through a Jerry Warren movie on late-night TV and was stirred into paying attention by Katherine Victor's "Dr. Myra" role in director Warren's otherwise Godawful **TEENAGE ZOMBIES** (1959, USA).

Tom Weaver notes on IMDb that Katherine was thankfully "always busy outside of acting (in modeling, real estate and in various jobs in the animated cartoon business)," but that "the stigma of being a regular in Warren's movies stymied her mainstream acting career."[24] Indeed. Nor did she make much of a "living" from Warren, or Tucker, for that matter, earning only a reported $300 from Warren for her pivotal role in **TEENAGE ZOMBIES** and a whopping $450 from Tucker

24 http://www.imdb.com/name/nm0896124/bio?ref_=nm_ov_bio_sm

Both titles for Katherine Victor's only starring vehicle for Jerry Warren (1966); the title change was prompted by legal threats from DC Comics!

Before **THE CAPE CANAVERAL MONSTERS,** an alien energy-lifeform reanimated the dead Dr. Van Ponder (Richard Devon) to foil mankind's first space launch in Roger Corman/ Irving Block/Jack Rabin/Lawrence L. Goldman's first-to-the-boxoffice Sputnik spinoff **WAR OF THE SATELLITES** (1958)

for **THE CAPE CANAVERAL MONSTERS** one year later. She went on to appear in the "bonus footage" shot for Warren's US cut-and-dubbed/padded editions of **RYMDINVASION I LAPPLAND** ([1959] a.k.a. **INVASION OF THE ANIMAL PEOPLE,** 1962; see *M!* #9, pp.5-16]), and **LA MARCA DEL MUERTO** ([1961] a.k.a. **CREATURE OF THE WALKING DEAD,** 1965), which I'll be writing-up for *Monster!* down the road.

Katherine also appeared in Warren's recuts of **CURSE OF THE STONE HAND** ([1964] incredibly cobbled-together from *three* 1940s Chilean movies directed by Carlos Hugo Christensen) and **HOUSE OF THE BLACK DEATH** ([1965] with Warren finishing a feature abandoned by director Harold Daniels), as well as the infamous **FRANKENSTEIN ISLAND** (1981, both USA), Warren's final film. However, Katherine Victor will forever be enshrined by many for her titular role in Warren's gobsmacker **THE WILD WORLD OF BATWOMAN** (1966), and far be it from me to steal any thunder

from her there. She's went on to work in children's television and animation for Disney(!) and others, initially as a production and/or continuity coordinator (as "Kathrin Victor") for series like *TaleSpin* (1990-91), *Darkwing Duck* (1991-92), *Goof Troop* (1992), *Bonkers* (1993-94), *The Little Mermaid* (1992-94), *Quack Pack* (1996), *Jungle Cubs* (1996), *101 Dalmations: The Series* (1997-98), *Timon & Pumbaa* (1996-99), *Hercules* (1998-99), and the Pixar **TOY STORY** spinoff series *Buzz Lightyear of Star Command* (2000-01, all USA), among others.

What would Buzz Lightyear have made of Hauron and Nadja?

It is with great respect and deep affection that I write: Katherine Victor will always be the greatest space-zombie of them all, Nadja, to me…

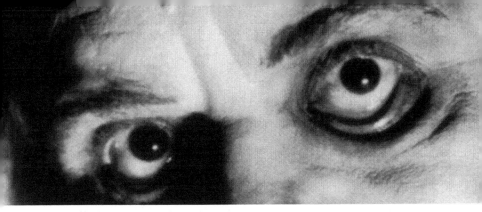

LONDON AFTER MIDNIGHT:
Lon Chaney, Tod Browning & Lost Films in Australia

by Daniel Best

*On a personal note – The author remembers seeing the uncut version of **FRAN-KENSTEIN** (1931, USA) in 1982. Here's how it came about: In the early 1980s, a retired cinema projectionist began to screen movies at a local theatre on Sunday evenings during the winter months. The movies were obtained by him when film runs had ended. Instead of throwing the films out, he kept them and stored them in a barn. In this way he was able to screen movies that are now thought to be lost, including **LONDON AFTER MIDNIGHT** (1927, USA), which the author remembers seeing in 1981. (From "Frankenstein, The Australian Connection – Part One" in* Monster! #15 [p.23, endnote #14])

With those words, this author recently opened a can of worms. After the publication of my two-part "Frankenstein, The Australian Connection" series in *Monster!* [*which began in issue #15 and concluded in #17 – ed.*], I was attacked on a number of forums by some very eminent historians, fans and authors, the bulk of whom have accused me of lying for my own gain. As I donated the articles to *Monster!*, I gained nothing, nor did I want to. I stated a fact: that the long-lost **LONDON AFTER MIDNIGHT** was still in existence, in Australia, in 1981. One of the claims put forward was that, as all films were returned to the production company (in this case, MGM), then **LONDON** could not have remained in the country. Other claims were that Chaney was not popular in Australia and that **LONDON** only had a limited run. This article will show that none of those claims are true!

What follows is a short summary of the history of lost films in Australia and how movies that are no longer in existence in countries such as America might well still be intact here. The article will also show that lost movies are found here, including MGM films thought to be gone forever after the negatives and prints were burnt in the famous MGM film fire of May 1957.

Let us begin…

The number of "lost" movies that are still sought after is legion, and the list is not restricted to American silent films. Titles from all over the world—including America, England, Australia and Russia—are now on a list of lost movies. Virtually any country that has had a film industry boasts of lost movies, and they range from silent shorts from the beginnings of cinema through to the 21st Century,

Top: US tradepaper announcement (circa 1915) and a still for the long-lost American horror film **LIFE WITHOUT A SOUL** (*above*)

although the advent of digital filmmaking and easier duplication of work prints and rushes now limits the amount of films that get lost.

Amongst the top of the list are films such as the comedy short *Humor Risk* (1921, USA, D: Richard Smith), which marks the first film outing for the Marx Brothers. **LIFE WITHOUT SOUL** (1915, USA, D: Joseph W. Smiley) is also high on everyone's want-list, if only because it represents the first full-length adaptation, albeit unofficially, of Shelley's *Frankenstein* (the Edison version, made in 1910, lasts for just 12 minutes). Films by major stars, both silent and into the talkie era, such as Clara Bow, Tom Mix, Norma Talmadge, Louise Brooks, W.C. Fields, Mary Astor, Gloria Swanson, Dorothy Gish and Claudette Colbert, along with the screen debuts of (the future Lord) Laurence Olivier, Robert Donat, Errol Flynn, Sophie Tucker, Irene Dunn and (the future Sir) John Gielgud are now also considered lost.

Two films stand head and shoulders above others though, both made and released in 1927. Hal Yates' short *Hats Off* is considered to be a Holy Grail of comedy, starring Stan Laurel and Oliver Hardy. The last reported screening of the movie was in Germany in mid-1930, after which all prints vanished without trace. The second film is the now-legendary **LONDON AFTER MIDNIGHT**, a horror/mystery starring the legendary Lon Chaney and directed by the enigmatic Tod "**DRACULA**" Browning, making his first excursion into the world of vampire horror, for which he would become immortal.

LONDON AFTER MIDNIGHT has been listed as a lost film since a fire raged through the MGM film vault on May 13, 1967. Hundreds of silent films were totally destroyed in the fire, along with early MGM cartoons, films made by Laurel and Hardy and The Three Stooges (although the lost Stooges film, as will be revealed, has since been found, in Australia), plus various *Our Gang* short features. The cause of the fire has long been attributed to the rather volatile nature of nitrate, a chemical that was in wide use in film in the early part of cinema.

The Effects of Nitrate Use in Film

The common problem with nitrate film is that it deteriorates when exposed to air over the years. Stories abound of film canisters being opened only to reveal either dust or heavily decayed film, which cannot be restored. Nitrate was in common use, in film, until 1951 when it was replaced by film with an acetate base. The acetate film was more stable and tended to last longer, resulting in less films being lost since.

Nitrate film had another, more sinister flaw. The camphorated cellulose nitrate base used in film was highly unstable and could—and often *did*—catch fire, resulting in serious injuries, property loss and, in some cases, loss of life. Australia wasn't immune to cinema fires. The dangers of nitrate film in Australia were identified almost at the same time as film was imported. In May 1897, a fire broke out at the Bazaar of Charity in Paris, resulting in the loss of an estimated 150 lives; an incident which is regarded as the first major cinema fire. Shortly after this disaster, and days before a public display of the Edison Vitascope in Adelaide, South Australia, the then-Fire Superintendent, George Brooker, called for an official clause to be inserted in the Places of Public Amusement Act, writing, "The celluloid films burn with great ferocity and once a mass of these become ignited it is impossible to extinguish them as it would be to subdue a heap of gun cotton which had caught fire." Brooker then went on to point out that gun cotton was an ingredient in nitrate film, and that he had personally observed a blaze of over 50 feet in height caused by twenty such reels. Brooker's submission was not addressed until 1902, when the argument for the insertion of the clause was discussed.

Cinema fires were being reported in Australia as early as 1905, when the Narrabri Town Hall burst into flame, resulting in the loss of films and other property damage. The cause of the fire was put down to a leaking gas pipe. The fumes were ignited by the limelight of the projector and the film itself then went up, causing a stampede. Fortunately nobody was hurt by the blaze, although minor injuries were reported due to people tripping over seats in the rush to escape.

The reportage of cinema fires in Australia sometimes reads like a Keystone Kops scenario, as evidenced by a 1909 fire at the Darlington Central Hall. An estimated 500 people escaped injury when film combusted and thick black smoke engulfed the hall. The most serious injuries in that fire came when the fire wagon collided with a tram, throwing a wheel and causing the horse to panic, resulting in firemen being hurled into the street, causing concussions. In 1910, the town hall in Forbes in country New South Wales exploded when film went up due to an unattended cigarette. Again, there were no injuries but the hall was partially demolished by flying bricks, some of which went through the roof and landed meters away, and a large hole was made in the wooden floor.

Jocularity aside, Australia was lucky in that nobody was killed, or seriously injured, in cinema fires during the early part of the 20th Century. Injuries were generally confined to women fainting and men being knocked down in the rush to escape the theatres or town halls. Fires might be started by sparks from the projector, stray cigarettes being thrown into film cans or general inexperience in the process of projection. One fire, at Balmain in 1910, was caused when the 14-year-old projectionist became so caught up in watching the movie he was showing that he didn't notice the film getting overheated.

On New Year's Eve, 1912, a fire started in the Crystal Palace Picture Theatre on George Street, Melbourne, resulting in the complete loss of dozens of short and feature films. The cause of the fire was put down to spontaneous combustion, as the fire was believed to have started in the film room; the most likely culprit was nitrate film. Once the first film canister went up, other film, which would normally be in open canisters, or spooled and waiting, ready to go, would have resulted in an impressive, if destructive, conflagration.

March of 1912 saw another fire that had the potential

EXPLOSION IN TOWN HALL.

FORBES, Monday.
Whilst preparations were being made at the Town Hall this afternoon for a cinematograph entertainment billed there to-night in aid of the funds of the local cricket ground, an explosion occurred. Bricks were hurled through the ceiling with great force, and a hole was also made in the floor. No one was injured. The show was abandoned.

Top: Nitrate-based film can be hazardous to your health! Australian newspaper item (from *SMH* for February 22, 1910). **Above:** Queensland newspaper ad (from *The Morning Bulletin* for August 22, 1928)

to cause a major disaster. The film library of Universal Films Limited, located on Pitt Street, Sydney, went up, resulting in an explosion. The flames quickly spread, and only prompt action by firefighters prevented the fire from burning down Pitt Street. As it stood, neighboring buildings were affected by both flame and smoke, and water damage was rife. It is unknown as to the extent of the loss of film, but, luckily, there was no loss of life nor any reports of major injuries.

Other countries weren't so lucky, however, as the volatile nature of nitrate film resulted in a number of devastating tragedies. A cinema fire in St. Petersburg in March, 1912, claimed the life of 90 people. In Paris, a year earlier, the death toll was 35. The Spanish city of Villa Real saw a cinema fire in 1912, resulting in 86 dead. The fatalities kept coming well into the 1920s: for example, a timber barn used as a cinema in Dromcollogher, Ireland, burnt to the ground, killing 48 people in September 1926 after a candle ignited a reel of film. As late as New Year's Eve 1929, another cinema, this time in Paisley, Scotland, was the scene of a nitrate film disaster when a reel of film began to emit thick black smoke after being placed into a can. The resulting smoke caused a stampede which saw 69 children die, along with two adults.

Something had to be done to ensure the safety of patrons, though, and legislation was quickly drawn up and put into action in 1914; but by 1920 it was woefully inadequate and out of date. The original legislation included such safety precautions as a minimum clear space between the projector and the audience, the use of electric light or miner's safety lamp, but not naked gas or oil flames or matches, and that a wet bag or blanket and a bucket of water must be kept readily available. This wasn't always adhered to, as official inspectors had to give notice before they inspected and a bucket of water could always quickly be brought in. Other recommendations did have an immediate effect, with the cessation of the use of naked flames in projection rooms reducing cinema fires dramatically.

Australian Cinema & Imports

The early years of Australian cinema were a free-for-all. The first film to be screened in Australia was in August 1896 when Carl Hertz gave a demonstration of the kinematograph at the Melbourne Opera House. This exhibition came less than a year after the first public exhibition of moving pictures by Lumières in Paris. After this, screening cinema took off, with moving pictures being shown as a novelty in vaudeville acts between live shows. The Australian film industry began shortly after, and more shorts were being made mere weeks after the first screening in 1896.

When it came to exhibiting foreign films, local distributors would import film to be shown around the country, until American film companies, realizing the financial potential that existed, began to establish companies and subsidiaries in the country. Importers such as Famous Lasky Film, Fox Film Corporation, Mutual Film Exchange, United Artists (Australia), First National Pictures Service and others all were quickly formed and aligned with their corresponding American studios.

Universal Films Limited was established, and funded by a public float, in early 1923.[1] *[see endnotes below]* This company controlled the rights to Universal Pictures (USA), along with Biograph. Eventually Universal Pictures would take control of Universal Films Ltd.; during the 1927 Royal Commission the head and founder of Universal Films Ltd., the delightfully named Hercules McIntyre, swore under oath that his company was the official Australian representative of the American company.

By 1920, new legislation had been enacted that made the storage and usage of film safer. Film houses had to be designated as such, whereas before a town hall might be used as a makeshift cinema at random, and every film house had to pass stringent safety checks before they could exhibit.

Newspaper ad (from *The West Australian* for November 3, 1931) advertising, amongst other things, a "Monster Children's Party" (*yes!*) and a Sunday showing of **LONDON AFTER MIDNIGHT** [*lower right corner*]

Each state had their own variations, though: in Queensland, a cinema could not operate on Sundays; in Tasmania a license was required. Western Australia required an inspection by the Department of Health before any cinema could be opened. The result was a mishmash of rules and regulations across the board which changed from year to year as various Governments, both state and federal, tried to keep up with a booming new medium.

One aspect of cinema that bothered many was the importation of American films. Tariffs were not introduced until 1914, and before this date, any film, exposed or not, could be imported into the country duty-free. The first duty to be imposed, after 1914, was flawed. The duty was a flat fee, based on the length of the film. This meant that a Charlie Chaplin short would cost the same as an educational short, regardless of the profit that was available. In 1918, a second tariff was introduced. This one required that an estimate of the total profit be supplied, against which duty charges would be applied.

There was a loophole, though. A little-known clause in the legislation meant that an American studio could sell a film to its Australian agent outright. American companies soon realized that, by charging more in costs than a movie was estimated to make, they paid zero taxes in Australia. This resulted in a windfall for them, and a loss, of sorts, for the local distributors. The "loss" was offset by the charges that the distributors placed onto films for the various movie chains—companies such as Hoyts would pay the distributors a premium price, this would then be recouped by ticket sales. That the movie would make more than the original estimate was a furphy *[Australian slang for a false report or rumor – ed.]*; by that stage, the money was already in America and the tax wasn't able to be enforced.

Another issue was quotas. As the American film industry took off, more and more product was becoming available. In its own way, film was cheap to exhibit for theater managers. There were none of the costs that would normally be incurred by engaging a troupe of vaudevillians, and the glut of movies meant that the program could be changed on a weekly basis, if not more often. This meant that film was aimed squarely at working men, women and children. The higher classes were still more interested in live theater. As the amount of film imported increased, the local industry decreased. Australia, one of the world leaders in filmmaking in the first years of the 20th Century, was virtually wiped-out by the end of the 1920s. The new quotas allowed for a certain amount of American film to be imported, along with unlimit-

Top: This Hispanic poster may be Mexican, or else for Latino audiences in the USA.
Above: This Belgian poster indicates that **LONDON AFTER MIDNIGHT** did get exported to Europe, so perhaps a print might be turned up there someday

ed amounts of British film. This was remedied in 1933 when legislation was again amended to protect the local industry, albeit a tad too late. By the end of the 1920s, it was reported that 90% of all film imported into Australia originated in America.

In The Midnight Hour: You'd be saying your prayers too if you saw this freaky fellow standing at your bedside in the middle of the night! *[Editor's Note: I scanned this striking image from a modern, standard-sized sepia-tone postcard ("Fotocard") that I bought in Toronto decades ago, which was issued circa the 1980s on into the '90s (?) by Ludlow Sales of New York. I've never seen another copy of this same postcard or still anywhere else either before or since, so it's well worth running here due to its evident rarity. Enjoy, Lonsters! – SF]*

The Importing Process & Non-Returns

When it came to the physical importing, the process was simple. American film companies would take a negative of their movies and then strike positive films for exhibition. These films would then be sent, via boat, to Sydney (where the bulk of the film companies had their head offices) and loaned out, at a cost, to cinema chains, and then be returned to the studio in question afterwards. If the movie was deemed to be a popular one, such as a Chaplin, Fairbanks or Pickford feature or short, then up to 40 prints would be sent over. If the movie was of limited value, anywhere from only one to no more than five (one for each major state) would be shipped out. In this way, Australia was always a few months—if not more—behind America when it came to a film's debut.

An important aspect to the Australian experience was that film was not required to be returned to America. Once a film had finished its run, the cinema would send it back to the state distributor, who would then store the film for further rentals. In some cases, film positives were struck from the positives sent from America; these copies, technically pirates, were generally sent out to country regions. Once the film went to a country center, the distributor often forgot about it. If it was a film that

was a few years old, then that film would be stored at the cinema, or yet another copy was made. The result of this was that, if an American studio were to audit the distributor, then all would be in order as they'd never ask about any copies.

Films were also provided to Picture Show Men.[2] These itinerant men would purchase films outright from studios and film processing laboratories and then travel the countryside and outback regions of Australia, showing the films in town halls, churches and even tents to small-town locals. These films were used and abused to the point of destruction, and if a film were to become damaged, then the Picture Show Man would often just cut the film and splice it, creating a "new" version. The advent of sound made this cutting harder, but not impossible, to do. It wasn't unusual for a Picture Show Man to keep all of his stock, storing them in barns and attics when they were no longer required.

Films were also duplicated for decades by projectionists showing the movies. These duplicates, along with cast-off films from distributors and film studios, would often find their way into private collections, as they were considered to be of zero value as assets. As such, by the 1950s and certainly the 1960s, it wasn't unusual to find retired projectionists and cinematographers with home cinemas complete with a personal library of features and short films.

Lon & Louise, Chaney & Lovely

When it comes to lost films of major stars, Lon Chaney arguably suffers the most. Of the estimated 155 films that he was credited in, approximately 109 of those are now lost, with the most famous being **LONDON AFTER MIDNIGHT**. This leaves just 46 films that are still extant, and some of those are mere fragments, consisting of minutes of footage. The bulk, if not all, of Chaney's pre-1920 films were released in Australia. Advertisements exist for early films such as **DAMON AND PYTHIAS** (1914, D: Otis Turner), **THE GRIP OF JEALOUSY** and **THE GILDED SPIDER** (both 1916, D: Joseph De Grasse). Chaney at first became known to Australian audiences, not for his acting ability, or his skill with makeup, but through his association with Australian actress Louise Lovely.

Born in Sydney, Nellie Louise Alberti was already an established actress when she left Australia for success in Hollywood. Arriving in America, the now-married Louise Welch[3], to much chagrin, was quickly renamed Louise Lovely by none other than Universal Studio head Carl Laemmle, and was placed into films as the lead competition for Mary Pickford. Lovely's co-star for her early films was a young Lon Chaney, and her Australian heritage ensured that her films were rushed into cinemas across the land, generally with her name being the only one mentioned. Louise Lovely's popularity as a local-lass-made-good ensured that Chaney's early feature-length efforts were seen by many. It also meant that all of the press attention, review-wise, was centered around Lovely, without any mention of her co-stars. It mattered not, though: Louise Lovely's films were popular and, by virtue of association, Lon Chaney built a steady following.

Chaney's name first appeared in print in Australia in 1916 when the short movie *The Trust* (1915) was released and it was noted in ads that Chaney both starred in and produced the short. From this point on Chaney was mentioned in some ads, but it took until he began to appear in feature-length films for his name to become known in its own right.

Chaney's career was already well-established as the 1920s were ushered in. A biography[4] appeared as early as 1922, to coincide with the release of **THE TRAP** (D: Robert Thornby), mentioning his early work but omitting his co-star, Louise Lovely. By this time Lovely had been dropped by

The aptly-named Louise Lovely (née Nellie Louise Corbasse a.k.a. Alberti), Lon Chaney's early Australian co-star

Universal after she asked them for more money. After being picked up by Fox, she made a series of now-lost, and, by all accounts, highly forgettable westerns before returning to Australia in 1924. Lovely set up her own film company, The Louise Lovely Production Company, in 1925, and promptly co-produced/co-directed (with Wilton Welch) and starred in a locally-made film, **JEWELLED NIGHTS**. This movie, itself also lost[5], fell victim to the haphazard film distribution process that was in place in Australia, and lost money. It proved to be her swansong and she retired from movies, passing away in 1985. As it stands, Lovely was a true pioneer of the Australian film industry, being one of the first locals to build a career in America and also, along with the multi-talented Lottie Lyell, one of the first Australian-born female producer-stars.[6]

Hunchback Claims A Victim

At the same time as Lovely was giving up on America and travelling back to Australia, Chaney was appearing in the movie that would make him a household name worldwide. **THE HUNCH-BACK OF NOTRE DAME** (1923, USA, D: Wallace Worsley) was announced to Australians in glorious full-page advertisements, with Chaney's name in small, albeit bold, type. The

BOY HANGED.

Bright Lad's Tragic End.

MELBOURNE, To-day
The death of Donald William McConnell (aged 11 years), of Caulfield, who was found hanged in a building in the course of erection, was enquired into by the Coroner (Mr. D. Berriman) yesterday.

Donald Malcolm McConnell, father of the boy, said that young McConnell was a bright lad. He had witnessed the moving picture "The Hunchback of Notre Dame," and had been impressed with the scene which depicted the hunchback sliding down a long rope to rescue a girl. It was possible that he met his death trying to copy the feat of the hunchback.

The Coroner found that the boy died from strangulation accidentally caused.

Top: Australian newspaper ad (from *The Brisbane Courier* for December 27, 1924; art by Ellen Farquhar). **Above:** Tragic accident as a young lad attempts to imitate The Hunchback and kills himself (South Australian newspaper item from *The Sunday Journal* for October 17, 1925)

Tivoli in Brisbane trumpeted the fact that their tickets would remain at their standard price, unlike cinemas in America, who increased theirs. They also announced a very welcome feature: an early form of cinema air-conditioning. **HUNCHBACK** was released in the summer of 1924. Most cinemas proudly announced that, for longer, feature films, oscillating fans would be installed to ensure the comfort of patrons.

HUNCHBACK was widely praised as a cinematic masterpiece, but the film was touched by tragedy. Shortly after its October 1925, release in Melbourne, Victoria, 11½-year-old Donald McConnell was found dead in a house on Kooyong Road, Caulfield.[7] McConnell had been taken to see **HUNCHBACK** and was enthralled by the film, in particular the scene where Chaney slides down a rope. The Victorian State Coroner found that McConnell was probably trying to emulate Chaney when he entered a house under construction with other boys, found a rope tied to the roof and tried to slide down it, only to have the rope twist around his neck several times, strangling him. By the time he was found, two hours later, McConnell was dead. His father, also named Donald, later stated that young McConnell was a bright, happy boy who had no reason to commit suicide. The result of this unfortunate death was that **HUNCHBACK** was quietly removed from Victorian cinemas for a period of time, although it was not officially withdrawn.

Chaney, a Household Name

Chaney's magnum opus came when **THE PHANTOM OF THE OPERA** (1925, USA, D: Rupert Julian) was released in 1926. Appearing as the titular character, Chaney created a character that is still capable of creating shock, even 90 years later. Unlike **HUNCHBACK**, only eighteen months earlier, Chaney's billing in ads was prominent, and larger than anyone else's; which was fitting as he was not only the star, but also co-directed the film, uncredited (as were fellow co-directors Ernst Laemmle and Edward Sedgwick). The movie was a resounding success in Australia and, finally, Lon Chaney was just as big a name Down Under as he was in his homeland.

One sour note was hit with **PHANTOM**, though, with the film being banned in Tasmania during its initial run for being too horrific. This ban in certain Tasmanian cinemas by local cinema owners ensured that the film's run was limited in Hobart. It made little difference to the movie's popularity, but the more prominent Chaney got, the more attention his films received from other state and federal censors. The results were that both **HUNCHBACK** and **PHANTOM** were censored for Australian release, but, as these censored prints have yet to be rediscovered, it is unknown to what extent cuts were made.

Chaney's next movies, **THE UNHOLY THREE** (1925, D: Tod Browning), **THE TOWER OF LIES** (1925, D: Victor Sjöström/"Seastrom"), **THE BLACKBIRD** and **THE ROAD TO MANDALAY** (both 1926, D: Tod Browning), **THE UNKNOWN** (1927, D: Tod Browning) and others were all given wide releases and received good reviews and publicity. He was a name actor, and one that MGM Ltd. (Sydney) and Universal, along with cinema chains, knew that people wanted to see. As such his movies were constantly rereleased and placed back into circulation, with his most popular films, such as **HUNCHBACK** and **PHANTOM**, being shown in the country on an almost continuous basis. When **LONDON AFTER MIDNIGHT** was due for release, it was given good advance notices, along with Chaney's **LAUGH, CLOWN, LAUGH** (1928, D: Herbert Brenon), also due for release. Director Tod Browning was also showcased, on the strength of his above-cited Chaney collaborations.

Tod Browning –
An American (Not) In Australia

Tod Browning became one of Chaney's best-known and most sympathetic collaborators. The first movie that the combination of Chaney and Browning made was **THE WICKED DARLING** in 1919. From there on they continued to work at a rapid pace, producing a further nine movies in ten years, seven of which came in a four-year period. Out of the nine movies they made, **THE BLACKBIRD**, **LONDON AFTER MIDNIGHT** and 1928's **THE BIG CITY** remain lost and **WHERE EAST IS EAST** (1929) only survives incomplete. The remaining movies, aforementioned **THE WICKED DARLING**, **THE UNHOLY THREE**, **THE ROAD TO MANDALAY**, **THE UNKNOWN**, **WEST OF ZANZIBAR** and **WHERE EAST IS EAST** are all considered to be Chaney classics.

The films that Browning made with Chaney lifted his (Browning's) profile in the motion picture world and established him as a director who specialized in horror, thriller and suspense, with a penchant for more unusual subject matter than most. That Browning would make **LONDON AFTER MIDNIGHT** as a vampire film with Chaney came as no great surprise, and when it came time for Universal to make *Dracula* they looked no further than the team of Chaney and Browning. Sadly, Chaney would pass away before filming began, leaving a Hungarian stage actor, Bela Lugosi[8], to fill in for him. It's long been debated how a Chaney **DRACULA** would have looked, and it's easy to speculate that his Dracula would have been somewhat similar to his faux but fearsome-looking vampire in **LONDON**.

One aspect of Browning's career deserves investigation. It has long been said that Tod Browning toured Australia in 1912 as part of a double act in vaudeville. For years this tour was hard to confirm as the name of the act that he toured with is variously reported as being either *The World of Mirth*, *The Whirl of Mirth* or *The Wheel of Mirth*. An extensive search of touring acts during this time period does not divulge any of those titles, while another Browning show, *The Lizard and the Coon*, is also absent from records, and there is no mention of a Tod(d) Browning in contemporary news reports. The questions then remained, *did* Browning tour Australia, *what* was the source

Australian newspaper ad (from *The Newcastle Sun* for June 10, 1926)

85

This wonderful faux fan-art poster (by 4gottenlore @ Deviant Art) illustrates what might have been, but never came to be

of the information and, *if* it *did* happen, *when* did it happen?

Simply put, there is no evidence that Browning ever came to Australia in the early part of the 20th Century. According to historian and author of *The Secret World of Tod Browning*, David J. Skal[9], the information about the Australian tour came from Browning himself, who was prone to embellishing stories about his early career. The show, named *The Whirl of Mirth*, certainly did tour America in 1912, but Browning was back in Hollywood and working with

Australian newspaper ad (from *The Advertiser* for June 27, 1928)

D.W. Griffith in 1913, meaning that an Australian tour could not have happened. Skal also mentioned the fact that Browning first applied for a passport much later in life than *The Whirl of Mirth*, meaning he could not have toured Australia.

Further research supports David Skal's comments. In the first years of the 20th Century, an act from anywhere else in the world touring Australia was given a lot of exposure. Entertainment at the time was still geared towards live performances, mainly vaudeville, and it would remain that way until the mid-'Teens, when film would take over. An American vaudeville act in 1912 would have been featured prominently in newspapers, both in advertisements and features, as were vaudeville and variety shows featuring the likes of W.C. Fields (1903) and Houdini (1910) through to speaking tours by Mark Twain (1895) and Arthur Conan Doyle (1920). As soon as an overseas act was booked, it was promoted, no matter how obscure the cast.

Part of the reason for the media exposure was to increase the box office take. An American act was a novelty in Australia and, with the sheer amount of acts touring, something new and unique was a surefire way to bring people through the doors. It is inconceivable that an American vaudeville act could tour Australia in 1912 and receive no mention in any newspaper in the country.

London After Midnight & *"Lawrence" Chaney*

Although released in America in December 1927, **LONDON AFTER MIDNIGHT** wasn't released in Australia until April of 1928, whereafter it quickly traveled around from state to state. Much was made of the mystery of the detective story, with reviews making almost no mention of the vampire aspect of the film. Chaney, billed as "The Screen's Greatest Character Star" and "The Prince of Actors" was praised for his performance, and Browning's direction was also singled-out for its atmospheric and gothic overtones. On an amusing note, one regional New South Wales newspaper made mention of the movie starring "Lawrence" Chaney.[10] By the end of 1928, the film was being shown as a double-bill with Charlie Chaplin's latest hit **THE CIRCUS**, thus ensuring that the movie would be one of Chaney's most profitable Down Under.

It was at this time that Chaney was linked to another tragic death. News of a homicide in London involving the film, in early January 1929, made a sensation. Robert Williams, a 28-year-old male, was arrested, tried and convicted of cutting the throat of a housemaid in Hyde Park. During his trial, Williams claimed that he saw the face of Lon Chaney, resulting in a blackout. Of interest is that the character Williams claimed to have seen was none other than Quasimodo, Chaney's title role in **THE HUNCHBACK OF NOTRE DAME**. If Williams did indeed hallucinate this, then that would make *two* deaths which could be attributed to **HUNCHBACK**'s influence. The story had an even sadder ending. In 1933, the clearly mentally-disturbed Williams piled-up mattresses in his padded cell, climbed up onto them then leapt to the floor, fatally fracturing his skull. The verdict was that he had committed suicide out of guilt. This successful attempt came after two previous attempts failed.

The news of the housemaid's murder did nothing to dilute the popularity of Chaney. **LONDON** was kept in circulation, and subsequent films, such as **THE BIG CITY** and **LAUGH, CLOWN, LAUGH**, were released to much fanfare and excellent reviews. While those other movies were shown and then shelved, **LONDON** proved to be so popular that it was still screening when Chaney passed away in September 1930. Indeed, **LONDON** proved to be so popular on Australian screens that it was shown well into the 1930s; one of the few silent films to be exhibited on a routine basis during the talkie period.

After *London After Midnight*

Chaney would make a further six silent features after **LONDON** and one talkie, a remake of his and Browning's **THE UNHOLY THREE** (1930). Browning bowed out of the remake (which was directed by Jack Conway instead), and, sadly, Chaney was dead before the film was released.

Chaney passed away due to a throat hemorrhage brought on by an infection following a bout of pneumonia. He was also suffering from lung cancer. His only talkie was a tour-de-force in speech, with Chaney providing the voice for five separate characters, including a parrot and an old woman. His passing was news in Australia and his films remained in circulation, outlasting the man himself.

Browning went on to make the all-time classic horror film, **DRACULA** (1931), a movie that, it could be said, launched the Golden Age of Horror. It certainly launched the Universal Studios horror period. After making **IRON MAN**, a potboiler with an aging Lew Ayres and a young Jean Harlow, Browning made one of the most sensational movies ever, 1932's **FREAKS**. A story set in a circus, the film was nota-

Whether he's a real vampire or not, the one Lon played in **LONDON AFTER MIDNIGHT** is one creepy dude!

ble for using real-life so-called "freaks", and was so horrific that it was refused release in Australia and banned until the 1980s.

In 1935, Browning made one last return to the vampire/horror genre, making a thinly-disguised remake of **LONDON AFTER MIDNIGHT**, titled **MARK OF THE VAMPIRE**, for MGM, starring Bela "**DRACULA**" Lugosi as the vampire and also starring Lionel Barrymore and Lionel Atwill. A gothic masterpiece, it surpassed **DRACULA** in many aspects, but it would be somewhat of a swansong, as Browning would make only two more movies before turning his back on Hollywood forever after getting fed up with studio interference on his 1939 mystery, **MIRACLES FOR SALE**. He passed away in 1962.

Today Browning is known, primarily, for **DRACULA**. His Chaney movies are still released on the latest format, be it video, DVD, Blu-ray or as digital downloads. As with Chaney, Browning lives on, and his influence can still be felt in modern gothic horror films.

The 1938 New Zealand *London* Experience

Chaney—as was Browning—was just as popular in New Zealand as he was in Australia. **LONDON AFTER MIDNIGHT** saw release there in 1928, and it was still being screened at cinemas, as a feature, in late 1930. However, in 1938, a movie titled **LONDON AFTER MIDNIGHT** began to appear at cinemas once more. Might it have been the Chaney/Browning classic?

The answer is *no*.

As fascinating as it may be to believe that the film was still in active circulation in major cities as the 1940s were rolling around, it wasn't to be. In 1938, a short feature was made in England titled *London After Midnight*. Other than for its title, this film had absolutely nothing in common with the Chaney/Browning classic, and it was described as being, "...a most interesting short showing life in the great metropolis when the theatres have lowered the curtains. It is the city of amusements and interesting sidelights on this angle are shown." In short, the '38 *London After Midnight* was nothing more than a travelogue, although advertising claimed it to be the best short featurette ever made.

Finding Lost Films, MGM, *Hello, Pop!*, *Hollywood Party* & *London After Midnight*

...Which leads to the question, what is the likelihood of Chaney's and Browning's **LONDON AFTER MIDNIGHT** existing in Australia in 2015 and beyond? The answer isn't as simple as it might seem. Certainly there was a copy in South Australia in the early 1980s, but the whereabouts of that copy is now unknown. MGM undertook a major worldwide search in the '80s in an attempt to track down certain films; some were rediscovered, many others were not.

Despite the best efforts of film studios and historians, lost films still turn up in Australia and New Zealand to this day. In 2013, a Three Stooges color short, *Hello, Pop!* (1933, D: Jack Cummings), was discovered in a private collection, having been obtained from

Australian newspaper ad for **LONDON AFTER MIDNIGHT**

another collector of film back in the early 1950s. The same collector also had the only known surviving sound version of the MGM short *Hollywood Party* (1937, D: Roy Rowland).

Hello, Pop! was one of the films lost in the same MGM film fire in May of 1967 that claimed the last known American print of **LONDON AFTER MIDNIGHT**. Its discovery, intact and viewable, shows that nitrate prints (as in the case of *Hello, Pop!*), survive intact if stored in the right environments. **LONDON AFTER MIDNIGHT** was still on Australian screens as late as November 1931, meaning that prints were *not* returned to MGM in America following their original theatrical run, but were instead kept locally. Prints of the film would have been retained by MGM's Australian subsidiary until they were deemed to no longer be of value, after which they would have either been dumped, sold or taken by private collectors.

Historians often tend to underestimate the sheer amount of cinemas that existed in Australia in the first part of the 20th Century. In Adelaide and its surrounding suburbs alone there were over 140 separate cinemas operating between the years of 1896 to 1929. Other larger capital cities, such as Sydney and Melbourne, easily boast twice that number alone. Each cinema would have films, which could be ordered from the distributors and were rarely returned. The common practice to meet the rising demand was to have an unofficial duplicate made. These duplicates would then be sent out, and the projectionist would store the film while on location.

Adding to the mix is the many regional cinemas that existed in Australia throughout the 20th Century. Almost every regional town throughout the country had a cinema, or facilities at a town hall at which movies could be shown. Sadly, a lot of these cinemas no longer exist, and the disposal/dispersal of their film libraries is unknown. In most cases, the actual locations of the cinemas themselves have largely been forgotten and are almost impossible to trace. Most of the films and equipment was disposed of, some was saved, and yet more stories emerge of a building being pulled down or renovated, only for workers to discover canisters of film in various stages of decomposition.

Other films have turned up in collections since the 1970s. These include silent, nitrate era lost films such as **SALOMY JANE** (1914, Ds: Lucius Henderson, William Nigh), **THE STAIN** (1914, D: Frank Powell), the Harold Lloyd comedy short *Peculiar Patients' Pranks* (1915, D: Hal Roach), **SEVEN SINNERS** (1925, D: Lewis Milestone), and talkies such as **MAMBA** (1930, D: Albert S.

Lon Gone: Chaney and Marceline Day, in a spooky scene from one of the most-wanted lost films of all time, horror or otherwise. Might a print of **LAM** someday turn up Down Under? That remains to be seen. But where there's doubt, there's still hope, as the old saying goes…

Rogell). Boris Karloff's **THE GHOUL** (1933, UK, D: T. Hayes Hunter), was considered lost for decades until a copy turned up in Europe. In Australia, **THE GHOUL** was in circulation, at cinemas, until the late 1930s[11], after which it vanished, presumably into archives. It is not inconceivable that a copy of this film is also still in a private collection somewhere.

Film has been found underneath stages, seats, behind switchboards, in attics and cellars of old cinemas and theatres for decades now. Stories of survival include one of a rabbit trapper in outback New South Wales who, upon discovering film canisters in an abandoned barn in the outback, wrote a letter on the back of a jam label and sent a number of film canisters to the National Library. The canisters contained previously lost pre-World War II newsreels and silent shorts. Possibly the most famous of all finds happened in France in the early 1980s when historians David Robinson and Kevin Brownlow took possession of hundreds of cans of formerly lost Charlie Chaplin silents, including outtakes, rehearsals and unrealized snippets of films. All of this film was nitrate-based and had to be brought into England very carefully and restored. The footage found formed the basis of the three-part TV series, *Unknown Chaplin* (1983, UK,

Ds: Kevin Brownlow, David Gill).

Construction workers in Lane Cove, Sydney in the early 1980s came across a steel door, leading to a previously unknown structure. The room turned out to be a film storage library of the Fig Tree Studio. The studio was founded in 1936 by the Mastercraft Film Corporation and closed in 1952, the premises being used as a car factory from that point until 1980. The factory/studio was in the process of being demolished until the forgotten vault was uncovered. Hundreds of film canisters and equipment were written off as garbage and promptly loaded onto the back of a truck to be shipped off to the dump. Fortunately a council worker happened to see the film cans on the truck and, in scenes that would have been right at home in a Keystone film, gave chase until the truck stopped, whereupon the man seized the film cans which were duly sent off to the national Film and Sound Archive in Canberra.

The Film and Sound Archive can, and often does, tell stories of people asking if they'd be interested in boxes of old film. Most are beyond restoration, but some—or at least fragments thereof—can be saved, resulting in lost film and lost footage, even stills, being made available. Even the Archive itself is not immune. While their usual focus is Australian film, every so often someone rediscovers some theretofore believed lost American or British film languishing in storage. Not every lead can be fully followed up, however, and there are still many abandoned buildings dotted around the country in remote areas that could feasibly contain material, film, equipment and ephemera that has yet to be discovered.

In this regard, there is still hope that **LONDON AFTER MIDNIGHT**, along with other lost films, shorts and features, is just waiting to be (re)discovered...

SOURCES

BOOKS
Royal Commission on the Moving Picture Industry in Australia & Marks, Walter Moffitt, *Report of the Royal Commission on the Moving Picture Industry in Australia* (Canberra: Government Printer, 1928)

Bertrand, Ina, *Cinema in Australia: A Documentary History* (Kensington, N.S.W: NSWU Press, 1989)

Edmondson, Ray & Pike, Andrew, *Australia's Lost Films: The Loss and Rescue of Australia's Silent Cinema* (Canberra: National Library of Australia, 1982)

NEWSPAPERS
New South Wales:
Barrier Miner
Braidwood Dispatch
Cessnock Eagle and South Maitland Recorder
Daily Advertiser
Newcastle Morning Herald and Miners Advocate
Northern Star
Southern Record
Sunday Times
The Armidale Chronicle
The Newsletter – An Australian Paper for Australian People

Queensland
Daily Mercury
Daily Standard
Gympie Times
Morning Bulletin
Pittsworth Sentinel
Truth
Warwick Examiner and Times

South Australia
Daily Herald
Kapunda Herald
Peterborough Advertiser
News
Sunday Journal
The Advertiser
The Recorder
The Register

Tasmania
The Examiner
The Mercury
The North Western Advocate

Victoria
Frankston Standard
Punch
Table Talk
The Advocate
The Age
The Argus

Western Australia
Daily News
Geraldton Guardian
Kalgoorlie Miner

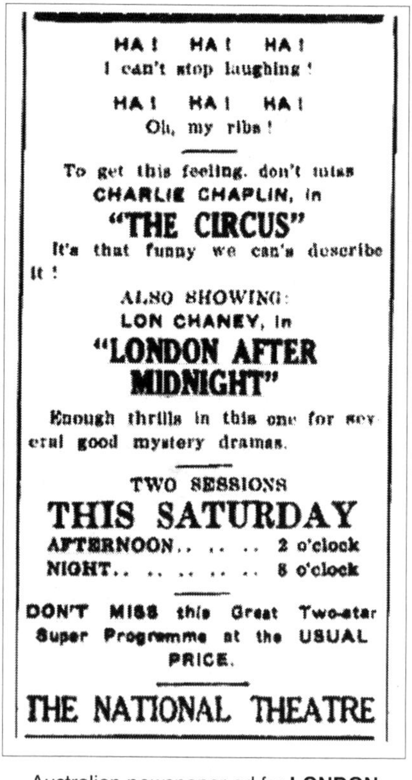

HA! HA! HA!
I can't stop laughing!

HA! HA! HA!
Oh, my ribs!

To get this feeling, don't miss
CHARLIE CHAPLIN, In
"THE CIRCUS"
It's that funny we can't describe
it!

ALSO SHOWING:
LON CHANEY, In
"LONDON AFTER MIDNIGHT"

Enough thrills in this one for several good mystery dramas.

TWO SESSIONS
THIS SATURDAY
AFTERNOON.. .. .. 2 o'clock
NIGHT.. .. .. 8 o'clock

DON'T MISS this Great Two-star Super Programme at the USUAL PRICE.

THE NATIONAL THEATRE

Australian newspaper ad for **LONDON AFTER MIDNIGHT**

Mirror
Sunday Times
The West Australian

New Zealand
Auckland Star
Evening Post
Hutt News
New Zealand Herald

(Endnotes)

1 The company, once aligned with Universal Pictures, was renamed Universal Film Manufacturing Company (Australasia) Limited in the early 1920s.

2 These exhibitors were the subject of a delightful 1977 Australian film, **THE PICTURE SHOW MAN** (D: John Power), based on the memoirs of a real Picture Show Man, Lyle Penn, and starring John Melion and Rod Taylor. As of this writing, a lovely HD widescreen upload of said film was viewable on YouTube (@ *https://www.youtube.com/watch?v=tlycZqRHUKI*).

3 Louise Lovely was known by many names in Australia. In addition to Louise Alberti, she was also known as Nellie Welch, Louise Welch, Louise Carbasse, Louie Kabash, Louisa Lovely and, in one memorable misspelling, Louise Lovel. Despite claims in fan magazines of the time, Lovely never took up American citizenship, stating so under oath before the Royal Commission into the Motion Picture Industry in Australia in June, 1927.

4 The Lon Chaney short bio was probably ghost-written

5 Only stills and a few photos of **JEWELLED NIGHTS** survive.

6 Women had a very active role in early Australian cinema. In addition to Lovely and Lyell, the most prominent of all female moviemakers down under are the McDonagh sisters. Paulette, Phyllis and Isabel ran their own studio and made films purely for the enjoyment of it, with Paulette as the writer-director, Phyllis the producer and Isabel the star (under the stage name of Marie Lorraine). And there was also Kate Howarde, who produced and directed silent films. Indeed Howarde's 1920 feature, **POSSUM PADDOCK** is considered to be the first full-length feature film written, produced and co-directed (with Charles Villiers) by a woman.

7 The actual house where McDonnell lived and the house next door where he was found dead have both since been demolished, and a block of units now stands on the location.

8 Browning had directed Lugosi a year earlier in **THE THIRTEENTH CHAIR** (1929, USA)

9 Correspondence between the author and David J. Skal, 6th December, 2015.

10 Chaney's real name was Leonidas Frank Chaney. Newspapers reporting his death gave his name as Alonzo, which was the name of a character that he'd played in **THE UNKNOWN** (1927).

11 **THE GHOUL**'s last verified screening was in January, 1937, when it was shown as a double bill, with **HIS BROTHER'S WIFE** (1936, USA, D: W.S. Van Dyke), starring Robert Taylor and Barbara Stanwyck, at the Centennial Theatre, Ballina, New South Wales. The movie was more than likely shown at other regional centers into 1940.

The earliest known Australian newspaper ad for a Lon Chaney movie which mentioned him by name ran in *The Townsville Daily Bulletin* (for March 9, 1916); the film advertised therein being Chaney's self-directed 1915 short, *The Trust*

MONSTERS AND VAMPIRES

SPINE-CHILLING CREATURES OF THE CINEMA
ALAN FRANK

Chris Lee was understandably one of the most commonly-seen horror icons depicted on the covers of 1970s genre reference books such as this one.

monsters, vampires & The erotic undead:
Remembering the '70s British Horror Hardcovers

by John Harrison

My parents took varying attitudes towards my mania for monster and horror movies when I was growing up. My dad dismissed them outright as "stupid", and couldn't understand why I would possibly want to read and learn more about them, let alone waste my time watching them (then again, my dad rarely understood any kind of hobby or interest that wasn't related to horse racing or golf!). But at least he wasn't like that awful father I had read about in *Famous Monsters of Filmland* #130 (December 1976), who scooped up all of his poor kid's monster magazines and Aurora kits and...*set them on fire!*

My mom, on the other hand, had a slightly more encouraging—or at least more tolerable—attitude. Unless it was on at too late an hour or I still had homework or chores to do, she never stopped me from watching any horror movies when they showed up on television. But the first time I realized that she was actually somewhat supportive of my "strange" interest was when I came home from school one afternoon and found a large hardcover book sitting on the dining room table, something which my mom had found at the department store that day and had bought for me as a surprise. The book was called *Monsters and Vampires*, written by a gentleman named Alan Frank, and I was immediately impressed that my mom had brought me home a book which featured a big, gaudy photograph of Christopher Lee on the cover, his eyes bloodshot and fangs bared in horror as his hands grapple with the wooden stake that has been plunged into his heart (a shot taken from Hammer's **DRACULA HAS RISEN FROM THE GRAVE** [1968, UK, D: Freddie Francis; see *Monster!* #13, p.29]).

While I had been buying *Famous Monsters* and other monster magazines for a while, and had found a few film tie-ins and other paperbacks like Edward Edelson's slim 1974 volume *Great Monsters of the Movies*, *Monsters and Vampires* was the first real book on horror movies that I had

One of the many erotic images to be found in Pirie's *The Vampire Cinema*; this one is a scene from Rollin's **THE SHIVER OF THE VAMPIRES** (*Le frisson des vampires*, 1971, France). The same image later appeared on the cover of Glitter/Creation Books' *Psychedelic Sex Vampires: Jean Rollin Cinema* (2012), by Jack Hunter

CONTINUED ON PAGE 97

MONSTER BOOK GALLERY

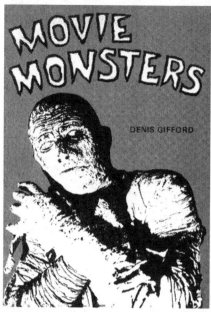

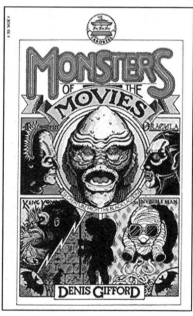

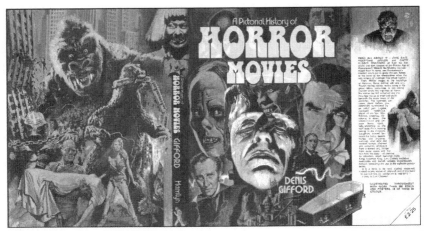

Above: Tom Chantrell's spectacular wraparound dust jacket art for one of the 1970s' most seminal horror movie tomes

Above: One of Gifford's glossy, full-color, oversized if slim 1990s softcover collections of Brit sci-fi comic art. **Left, Top to Bottom:** Gifford's pioneering 1973 tome was reprinted in a far-less-memorable new jacket design in 1984; Another Hamlyn horror hardback (1979) from the same decade, first published in paperback by Beaver in 1977

95

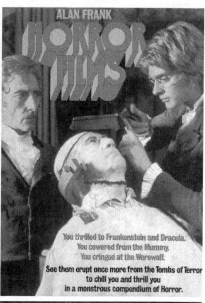

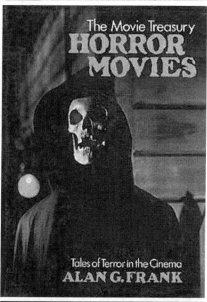

Clockwise, from Top Left: *Every Home Should Have One!* Another key '70s hardback horror book, which Octopus Books also issued in a different dust jacket design; another of Frank's numerous genre books, this one from 1976; Gifford's 1991 softback color comic art collection; Octopus' alternate jacket design. **The Men Behind The Pen:** The prolific Alan Frank *[left]*, circa 2012

70s MONSTER MEMORIES

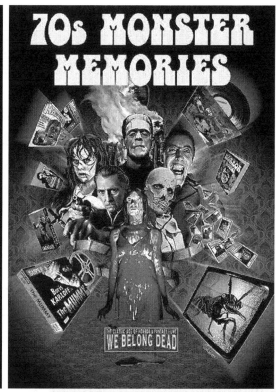

We Belong Dead's new tribute book. In 30-odd years, it too shall likely be a beloved classic, as are many of the '70s books cited here

WE BELONG DEAD

THE CLASSIC AGE OF HORROR & FANTASY FILMS

CONTINUED FROM PAGE 93

ever gotten my hands on, and considering the amount of time it got read and kept me quiet and entertained, I'm sure my mom thought it was well worth the few dollars I imagine she paid for it. First published by the London-based Octopus Books in 1976, the book certainly wasn't any kind of definitive history of horror cinema, something that was obvious to me even as a 13-year-old, but rather a joyous celebration of everything genre cinema had to offer in terms of memorable monsters and the bloodsucking undead. The text was fairly breezy and lightweight, though the enthusiasm of author Alan Frank certainly showed, and it introduced me to a lot of titles to watch out for in the late-late movie listings of the TV Week, but mostly it was the visual layout of Monsters and Vampires that held my attention so much, its 160 pages filled with an eye-popping selection of large B&W (and sepia-tinted) stills from an amazing cross-section of genre films, as well as a few pages of beautiful color plates included throughout the book.

The Stuff that Dreams are Made of

A sample page from WBD's 70s Monster Memories

The Men Behind The Pen: David Pirie at the Neuchâtel International Fantastic Film Festival (NIFFF) in 2012

The son of a British colonial civil servant, Alan Frank was born in South Africa and moved to England in 1956 to train as a doctor, before a severe burn to his hand forced him into a new career as a copywriter, which would eventually lead to 30-plus years as a film reviewer for *The Daily Star*, as well as writing a multitude of movie books, many of which focused on the horror, sci-fi and fantasy genres. I would later obtain Frank's other hardcover book in "The

Master illustrator Tom Chantrell, the man behind the brilliant cover art for Denis Gifford's *über*-classic *A Pictorial History of Horror Movies*, circa the 1970s (see more of his work on pages 102-104)

Movie Treasury" series, *Horror Movies* (Octopus Books, 1974) and his larger-sized *Horror Films* (Hamlyn, 1977), as well as his softcover volume *Sci-Fi Now* (Octopus Books, 1978). I also had Philip Strick's hardcover *Science Fiction Movies* (Octopus Books, 1976), which was another of "The Movie Treasury" books[1], and, while they were all great and informative in their own right and featured some terrific photos, none of them had the same impact on me that *Monsters and Vampires* did, both in its choice of film coverage as well as its graphic design. It became the first in an unholy trinity of horror movie hardcovers, all published in the United Kingdom, which helped both fuel and define my developing obsession with horror movies (yes, I am proud to say I was obsessed with monsters, and saw it as nothing more than a safe and healthy hobby, certainly a lot more interesting and satisfying to me than playing football or cricket was).

The second horror hardcover to have a huge impact on me is another classic that is fondly remembered by many of my generation: *A Pictorial History of Horror Movies*, by Denis Gifford (1927-2000), which was published by Hamlyn in 1973. I discovered this book around 1978, sitting on the discounted table in the Myer department store book section. The lurid, glow-in-the-dark green tint of the cover, which featured an amazing piece of wraparound art which showcased some of the most famous cinema monsters, instantly commanded both my attention and my pocket money. I was so engrossed in the book that I blindly jumped on the wrong train to get home, ending up somewhere by the Port Melbourne beach, several miles away from where I lived, and without enough money left to catch the train back to the city. But I didn't care too much, it was a nice sunny Saturday and I happily walked home along the wide concrete path beside the beach, my face happily buried within the pages of my newest acquisition.

When I finally arrived home, I holed myself up in my little backyard bungalow bedroom and combed through the book more carefully. The cover art was stunning, up there with the best *Famous Monsters* Basil Gogos covers or Aurora monster model kit box art by James Bama. While the Alan Frank books made great use of a single dramatic movie still for their front covers, the cover to *A Pictorial History of Horror Movies* was like a classic movie poster or pulp paperback, dripping

---

1   Other titles in "The Movie Treasury" series published by Octopus Books were *Western Movies* (by Walter C. Clapham, 1974), Gangster Movies (by Harry Hossent, 1974) and *Thriller Movies* (by Lawrence Hammond, 1975).

with atmosphere. It was one of those covers that was cool and fun to study and identify all the featured monsters and the movies they appeared in. The artist responsible for this striking piece was British-born Tom Chantrell (1916-2001), the son of a trapeze artist who would become a prolific designer and illustrator of movie poster art for the UK market, with over 7,000 titles to his credit! Chantrell most notably illustrated a lot of the Hammer Horror posters (see pp.102-104), which made him a natural choice for providing the cover to Gifford's book (and perhaps helps explain why the back cover features a rather out-of-place-looking Raquel Welch from **ONE MILLION YEARS B.C.** [1966, UK, D: Don Chaffey], which looks to have been simply cut from Chantrell's original poster art and pasted onto the cover in order to give the book a little bit of sex appeal). Chantrell also provided a lot of the poster art for the *Carry On* films, as well as a lot of adult features too, in addition to designing a ton of great, lurid British campaigns for such cult genre flicks as Bert I. Gordon's **FOOD OF THE GODS** (1976, USA), Umberto Lenzi's seedy Italian jungle adventure **EATEN ALIVE!** (*Mangiati vivi!*, 1980), and a classic double-bill of Norman J. Warren's **SATAN'S SLAVE** (1976, UK) with "Alex Fridolinski"/Bo Arne Vibenius' infamous Swedish revenge shocker, **THRILLER** (*Thriller – en grym film*, a.k.a. **THEY CALL HER ONE-EYE**, 1973).[2]

In-between Chantrell's covers lay 216 pages in which Gifford took this young reader on a journey which delivered what was pretty much promised by the title: a wonderfully-illustrated trip through the history of horror cinema, from the silent days up until the early 'Seventies, with particular emphasis on—and reverence for—the Universal classics of the 1930s and '40s. The British-born Gifford had a lengthy and varied career as a writer, radio broadcaster, comic book artist and film/radio/comic book historian, and his *Horror Movies* tome was certainly a lot more educational to me in terms of information and production stories provided, and he was clearly a lot more critical of films than Alan Frank was, and seemed particularly dismissive of the Hammer films, of which he said:

"In quantity Hammer are fast approaching Universal, but in quality they have yet to reach Monogram. Meanwhile they can admire their Queen's Award for Industry and laugh all the way to the bank."

Though I didn't agree with Gifford's opinion on Hammer, I found it refreshing to read a different point of view, as opposed to the glossed-over gushing which usually filled the pages of *Famous Monsters*. It was a style and approach that soon helped lure me to publications like *Cinefantastique*, *Gore Creatures* (later to become *Midnight Marquee*) and back issues of *Castle of Frankenstein*, all of which cast a more critical eye over genre cinema, and even when condemning a movie they would usually produce a lot more in-depth production information and intriguing personal perspective than was found in *FM* and many of the other more lightweight monster magazines from that period.

The third and final book I would like to look at here, another one that was instrumental in opening my eyes to new areas of the horror genre to learn about and seek out, was *The Vampire Cinema*, by David Pirie (1953-), another wonderful Hamlyn publication that appeared in 1977. I bought this book while on Christmas vacation in 1978, when I went up to tropical Cairns in far North Queensland. My copy still has the stamp from Walker's Bookshop on the inside front cover ("86 Lake Street, Cairns"), and the price written in pencil ("$10.95", which

Another of *The Vampire Cinema*'s erotic illustrations, this one showing Jacqueline Sieger as "The Queen of the Vampires" in Rollin's **THE RAPE OF THE VAMPIRE** (*Le viol du vampire*, 1968, France)

2   The family of Tom Chantrell run a great website devoted to his cinema art, as well as selling some original work and promotional pieces from his archives. The site can be found @ : *www.http:chantrellposter.com*

I figure must have chewed-up quite a chunk of my vacation money!). More than any other horror movie book, *The Vampire Cinema* had a much more illicit tone of forbidden fruit about it. While quickly flicking through the book in the store, I noticed it contained quite a few photographs of naked women, most of them in situations that were clearly both horrific and erotic. I had never seen these kinds of stills in *Famous Monsters*! As I fumbled for my money to hand over the counter, I felt like I was trying to buy my first dirty magazine, and I worried that the sales clerk was going to tell me I was too young to buy it. But no one batted an eyelid as I happily handed over my cash. Of course, I had to be careful that my mom didn't see some of the photos that were in it, but I figured the title and cover alone would ensure she kept a disinterested distance.

The Vampire Cinema was an absolute revelation for me. A book on vampire movies that DIDN'T have a photo of Bela Lugosi or Christopher Lee on the cover, but instead had a sole image of a green-tinted (at least to me) vampire standing out against bold blood-red background (even the rear of the book's jacket was nothing but red). The cover photo turned out to be a still of Philippe Gasté from Jean Rollin's **REQUIEM FOR A VAMPIRE** (*Requiem pour un vampire*, a.k.a. **CAGED VIRGINS**, 1971, France). With quotations from Bram Stoker's *Dracula* (1897) used as each chapter heading, *The Vampire Cinema* opened my eyes and mind, as well as

The Men Behind The Pen: Denis Gifford in 1976, enjoying some high-quality reading matter

my burgeoning sexuality, to the surreal, erotic vampire horrors of Rollin for the first time, not to mention the likes of Spanish filmmakers Jess Franco and Paul Naschy, and José Larraz's Sapphic shocker **VAMPYRES** (1974, UK). Chapters devoted to "The Sex Vampire" (*"The ruby of their voluptuous lips"*) and "The Latin Vampire" (*"The blood is the life!"*) both titillated and fascinated me, reading about Mexican, Italian, French and Spanish vampire movies; which sounded so much more exotic and disturbing than the mostly American and British productions that I had been exposed to up until that point. And the choice of stills and poster art used to illustrate these foreign films, particularly the color images, hinted at the unique use of shadows and atmosphere, and the beautiful color palettes found in Rollin's films. I loved Pirie's writing style and take on whatever film he chose to cover, and I spent a lot of time later on trying to hunt down a copy of the Scottish-raised writer's equally-excellent earlier book, *A Heritage of Horror: The English Gothic Cinema 1946-1972*, first published in the UK by Fletcher & Son in 1973 and once described by Martin Scorsese as "the best study of British horror movies and an important contribution to the study of British cinema as a whole."

As much as I devoured the contents of *The Vampire Cinema*, I pretty much resigned myself to the fact that reading about all these curious European vampire flicks was likely all I was ever going to be able to do. In 1978, home video was still a few years away from reaching Australian homes, and none of the local television stations ever screened this kind of stuff, not even at the most ungodly hours (about the raunchiest Australian late-night television ever got in the sex-and-horror stakes was Hammer's **THE VAMPIRE LOVERS** [1970, UK, D: Roy Ward Baker]). Slowly, through grainy VHS dubs in the 1980s, then via official video releases through Redemption in the '90s, as well as regular late-night screenings of old Euro-horror films on SBS (Australia's multicultural television channel), I finally started seeing all of the foreign films I had first read about in *The Vampire Cinema*. I soaked them up and was rarely disappointed in them, though I would have loved to have first experienced them at a younger age, to see what kind of effect they may have had one me. Now, of course, you can watch all this stuff in hi-def at the mere touch of a Google search.

When I returned to school early the following year, each student in my new class had to prepare and deliver a talk on any subject we liked (with the teacher's approval, of course!). I chose to talk about science-fiction and horror movies, and on the day of the talk I stood at the front of the class with my small stack of magazines and books, including *Monsters and Vampires, A Pictorial History of Horror Movies* and *The Vampire Cinema*. As Mr. Molino, our little Italian room teacher, sat at his desk to the right and slightly behind me, I delivered my talk enthusiastically while holding up open pages from the books for my class to see. Always having had a slight sense of mischief and cheek in me, I naturally held open some of the raunchier pages of *The Vampire Cinema* for my classmates to appreciate, which led to numerous requests to borrow the book! (Requests which I always denied: my books were my most-treasured possessions then.) But I got a kick out of secretly treating my class to a peek at some naked female flesh while Mr. Molino, a devout Catholic who would go on extended rants about the dirty magazines being sold at the corner milk bar, sat at his desk blissfully unaware that I was corrupting his students. I even got an A- for my talk!

Of course, there were plenty of other books on horror cinema, both in hardcover and trade paperback format, published throughout this period. Many of them are excellent, some are genuine classic studies, and no doubt some of them influenced other fans in their own special ways. But for me, it will always be these three that I single out here as the most important tomes of my formative years as a film buff. Many of the classic British books discussed or mentioned herein are now covered in the massive new 400-page softcover book entitled *70s Monster Memories*, published by the folks behind *We Belong Dead* magazine and covering just about everything that a hardcore horror fan growing up in that decade—particularly those living in England *[Like me!* ☺ *– SF]*—would have been exposed to and devoured, including a look at the books of Alan Frank and Denis Gifford. While a pricey purchase at £35.00 (that's in UK pounds), it is certainly a beautiful labor of love, and a wonderful nostalgia trip down a dark and shadowy memory lane.

Monsters and Vampires, A Pictorial History of Horror Movies and *The Vampire Cinema* have all been reprinted many times and can usually be found on Amazon and eBay in varying conditions and at varying prices, but if you hunt around you shouldn't have to pay too much for nice-condition copies. *70s Monster Memories* is available from the *We Belong Dead* website (@ *www.webelongdead.co.uk*).

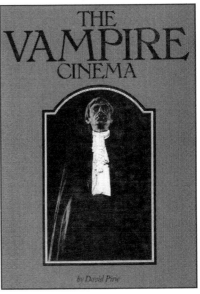

Top: W.H. Smith's 1988 edition (originally published by Hamlyn in 1984). **Above:** Who would ever have guessed that behind this restrained, dignified façade lurked so many nude lesbian vampire chicks!
[Editor's Note: When I found a remaindered copy of Pirie's TVC in a Toronto bookstore back in about 1989 or so, it came without a dust jacket, but was I ever thrilled to bits to find it anyway. And for only 5 bucks Canuck, too! – SF]

THE ART OF TOM CHANTRELL

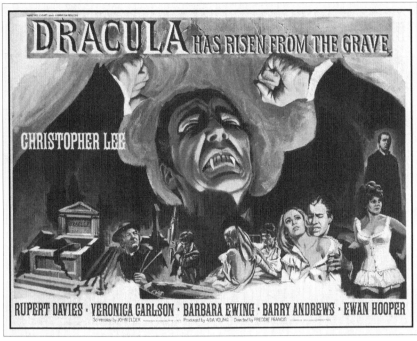

Above: UK quad poster

Above: Chantrell's titillating teaser poster for an unmade Hammer project, circa the early 1970s.
Right, Top to Bottom: THE DEVIL RIDES OUT;
DAWN OF THE DEAD (both are UK quad posters)

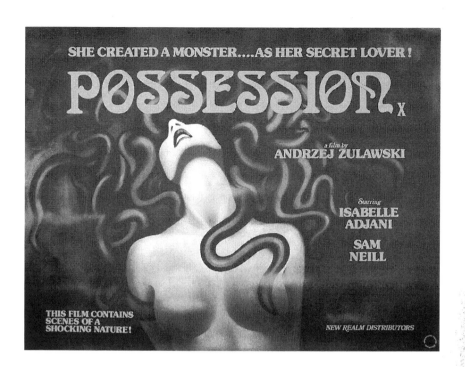

This Page and Next: A quartet of stunning British quad posters featuring Chantrell's bold and distinctive artwork

Another portrait of *Salem's Lot*'s Mr. Barlow, by Andy Ross

A wonderfully moody shot of Lugosi as the Count, down in the cellars of Castle Dracula with the coffins of his three vampire brides

THE MONSTER!
BOOK NOOK

Tod Browning's Dracula

Written by Gary D. Rhodes
Tomahawk Press, 2014
(*www.tomahawkpress.com*)
Price: $35.00 (US); £20.00 (UK)

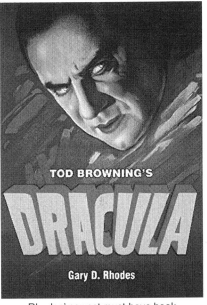

Rhodes' newest must-have book

Before 1930 there were no iconic images of Dracula. His name did not inspire fear and panic. Ladies did not swoon and faint dead away in his presence, and men did not tremble at the sound of his name. There had been a film bearing his name, Károly Lajthay's **DRAKULA HALÁLA** (1921, Hungary), starring Paul Askonas as Drakula, but this "lost" film was not a faithful adaptation of Stoker's 1897 novel, but only a thinly-veiled variation of it (some sources claim it wasn't even based on *Dracula* at all). A year later came **NOSFERATU** (*Nosferatu, eine Symphonie des Grauens*, 1922, Germany), F.W. Murnau's unofficial version of the Stoker novel, which would lead to his widow taking the film's producers to court to have all prints of it destroyed. **NOSFERATU** would receive its premiere in early March of 1922 at the Zoologischer Garten Berlin (Berlin Zoological Garden), of all places. *Variety* for April 21st, 1922 stated that it "was not worth all the shouting after all is said and done, a still-born Caligari. *[...]*" It may have been the first cinematic version of *Dracula* and be recognized as such to this day, but the Count's name was not used in either the promotion or as that of the film version's central character. (Furthermore, I can find no evidence that, at the time of its initial release, the film was released outside of Central/ Eastern Europe.) It can be assumed then that both British and American audiences would only have known the name either from reading the book or going to see the play, as was pointed out in *Silver Screen Magazine* in 1931: "*[...]* the title of the picture didn't mean a thing to anyone who hadn't read the book by Bram Stoker or seen the play". (Between 1904 through to 1914 there had been a "flexible aerialist / contortionist" bearing the name "Dracula", who toured the States; I can find no evidence whether or not his name had anything to do with Stoker's work, however.)

The play itself was causing some controversy in Britain, news of which *Variety* gleefully published on June 18th, 1924: "English Audience Horrified By Drama. *[...]* Dracula*, a dramatization of the late Bram Stoker's novel, was produced in a small country town, with remarkable results. Women fainted and men urged the actors to desist from their blood-thirsty conduct. *[...]* Edgar Allan Poe's weird stories pale beside it, reports indicate. *[...]* The future of the dramatization of *Dracula* is not known." Three years later in 1927, the play opened on Broadway, with Bela Lugosi taking to the American stage in the role that he would immortalize on the screen three years later. In October 1927, in a review of the play, *Variety* had this to say about Lugosi: "Bela Lugosi, dress-suited, used his dialect as the sinister Dracula, a clever conception all around."

As early as 1921 (or possible earlier), director Tod Browning was interested in developing the play for film: "Tod Browning recently threatened to 'Little Theaterize' the picture screen. "Dracula" was thought to be the 'Little Screen' possibility." Finally, in 1928, it was announced in the industry

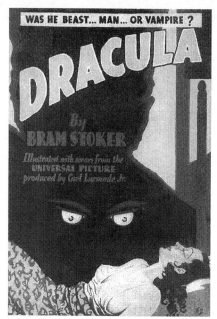

WAS HE BEAST... MAN... OR VAMPIRE ?

DRACULA

By BRAM STOKER

Illustrated with scenes from the
UNIVERSAL PICTURE
produced by Carl Laemmle, Jr.

Illustrated US hardcover tie-in edition for the 1931 film version

trade magazines that: "*[...]* Universal had bought the rights to *Dracula* and were going to make it '100 per cent dialogue and sound production,' with Conrad Veidt slated for the chief role of Count Dracula." (This was announced in at least

DE STAD
ANTWERPEN
EEN WEEKBLAD VOOR VLAANDEREN

IN HET NET GEVANGEN!

Contemporaneous Belgian magazine cover, dated 10 April, 1931 (roughly three months after the film had its stateside premiere)

three periodicals over three consecutive months.)

Finally, on February 14th (Valentine's Day), 1931, the world was formally introduced to Count Dracula on film when Lugosi first walked down the stairs of Castle Dracula and introduced himself with a thickly-accented "I am Dracula... I bid you *welcome*."

Audiences had never seen anything like it before—they were bombarded with images of decadence, power and immortality; young girls led astray and men corrupted and driven insane! The film was a huge box-office success, saving the financially-strapped Universal Studios from bankruptcy...and figuratively speaking it both created and destroyed its thereafter forever typecast star simultaneously!

"Bela Lugosi is playing the lead in Dracula. *[...]* He looks like Count Dracula. He is Count Dracula, the blood-sucking 'half-dead' vampire *[...]*" (Churchill, p.52).

For nearly 90 years, **DRACULA** (1931, USA) has stood as the first talking horror film, launching the first Golden Age of Hollywood horror cycle that roughly ended with **DRACULA'S DAUGHTER** (1936, USA, D: Lambert Hillyer). In October 1953, George Geltzer, writing an article on Tod Browning for *Films For Review*, would open the gates to the film's detractors, and negative criticism regarding it has been gaining in momentum ever since: "**DRACULA** was for years revered as perhaps the best-known of all vintage horror films, a sacred cow. *[...]* Time, alas has proved to be less kind to the film *[...]* Dracula is now widely regarded as the least satisfying of the Universal originals. *[It]* is now recognised as a film of missed opportunities" (Brunas, Brunas, Weaver, p.7).

So, while the films' detractors have been less than kind, all praise has been given to George Melford's Spanish-speaking version of *Dracula* that was filmed simultaneously to Browning's version, using the same sets.

Therefore, any serious study of Tod Browning's **DRACULA** would not only have to address the complaints and misrepresentations of its detractors, it would also have to do a scene-for-scene breakdown comparison between the two films as well as examine and answer the many myths and legends that have built up around the film—many of them perpetuated by Lugosi himself!

Now 60-odd years later, Lugosi historian and film scholar Gary D. Rhodes has entered the debate to confront and rectify the many "incorrect" stories surrounding **DRACULA** '31 that have been perpetuated since Geltzer's initial article cited above, many of which have taken on a life of their own due to being repeatedly reiterated by scholars/writers and more casual movie buffs alike. Rhodes gathers together all previously-published research and carefully dissects, reanalyzes and reevaluates each piece. Wherever the evidence does not support whatever claims, he amends it by showing the correct evidence.

For instance, Chapter 5 explores and discusses at length the long-held rumor that Karl Freund actually directed **DRACULA** (or most of it). This rumor was started by the film's heroic male lead David Manners, who was asked about the making of the film many years later, and due to certain of his "throwaway" comments made at that time, some historians have since latched-onto them and written about his unsubstantiated claims as though they were fact. The same chapter also compares the shooting script to the completed film. Chapter 4 illustrates how producer Carl Laemmle took great care over the film's scriptwriting and story development. Chapter 3 looks at pre-production and casting. Perhaps the biggest myth which surrounds **DRACULA** is that Lugosi was Universal's last resort for casting in the role of Count Dracula: a myth that he himself, of all people, perpetuated. In a 1939 interview for *The New York Post*, Lugosi said: "*[...]* dey start to test two dozen fellows for Dracula—but not me! And who was tested? De cousins and brodder-in-laws of de Laemmles *[...]* Dis goes on for a longk time and din oldt man Laemmle says, 'Dere's nobody in de family dat can play it, zo why don't you hire an egdor?'" (Cremer, p.116).

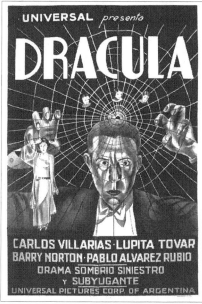

In his 1976 biography on Lugosi, Robert Cremer wrote about how, logically enough, Lon Chaney, Sr. was Universal's first choice for the role of Dracula. This was reiterated by David J. Skal in 1990: "The fact that Metro considered **DRACULA** with Lugosi and not Lon Chaney, whom they had under contract, is interesting and suggests that his director, Tod Browning, was fully aware of his star's failing health—Chaney

Right, Top to Bottom: Poster for the lost Hungarian "version" of *Dracula*, which may not have been based on Stoker's book at all; Argentine poster for the Spanish version of **DRACULA** '31 (art unsigned); NYC newspaper ad, circa February 1931

had throat cancer—so much so that he, and the studio, were willing to do **DRACULA** without their most bankable asset, the man of a thousand faces." (Skal, p.107); and in *Universal Horrors*: "*[...]* the unknown Lugosi was not Universal's initial choice for the Dracula role. The senior Chaney was of course the natural *[...]*" (Brunas, Brunas & Weaver, p.10). Precisely as to where this rumor originated is hard to define. In 1928 it was announced in various trade papers that Universal had bought the rights to *Dracula* and, as stated above, were planning to cast Conrad "**THE CABINET OF DR. CALIGARI**" Veidt in the title role. July 26th of 1930 saw the announcement that Tod Browning was to direct **DRACULA**, but "no cast selections or editorial assignments have been announced to date *[...]*" Exactly a month later, Chaney was dead of lung cancer. It could be speculated that, because Chaney and Browning had worked together numerous times, the horror

star would have been the logical choice to play the evil Count. Rhodes goes much deeper than this, pushing aside rumor and speculation that has long circulated as truth. He deals out historical FACT that lays to rest this story once and for all. Some people may disagree with his conclusions, but they are sound and are backed by historical evidence and not merely hearsay, speculation and/or rumor.

The book's chapters are: "The Vampire in America", "Tod Browning and Carl Laemmle, Jr.", "Pre-production", "The Script", "Production", "Post-Production", "Publicity", "Premiere", "General Release", "Reappearances", "Critical Backlash", "The Spanish-Language Dracula" and "Endings".

Through these chapters, Rhodes traces the complete history of **DRACULA** '31 from every conceivable angle. The book is beautifully laid-out and well-illustrated, and at 376 pages, it is the most in-depth study yet on one of the most iconic films of the 20th Century. This is Gary D. Rhodes' magnum opus, and it should be on every enthusiasts' shelf and in every film school's library. *10-out-of-10!* ~ **Matthew E. Banks**

©2015

"HORRIFIC"

Bela Lugosi, screen specialist in "horrific" parts, is at the King's Theatre this week in the dramatised version of Bram Stoker's vampire story "Dracula."

This sketch of Lugosi ran in Glasgow's *Evening Times* newspaper (June 18th, 1951), while he was touring the UK in a stage production of *Dracula*

References and sources
Variety (April 21st, 1922, p.43).
Silver Screen Magazine (June 1931, p.73).
Variety (June 18th, 1924, p.2).
Variety (October 12th, 1927, p. 50).
Motion Picture News (May 14th 1921).
Exhibitor's Daily Review (October 22nd, 1928, p.1).
Hollywood Filmograph (July 26th, 1930, p.12).
Brunas, M. Brunas J. & Weaver T. Eds. *Universal Horrors The Studios Classic Films, 1931 – 1946.* McFarland & Company, Inc., 1990
Cremer, Robert, *Lugosi – The Man Behind the Cape* (Henry Regnery Company, 1976).
Skal, D. J. *Hollywood Gothic: The Tangled web of Dracula from Novel to Stage to Screen* (W.W. Norton & Company, 1990).
Exhibitor's Herald World (October 18th, 1930. Churchill. "'Star Gazer' Heavy", p.52).
Hollywood Filmograph (May 24th, 1930, p.18).

THE STRANGEST PASSION EVER KNOWN!
"DRACULA"

MONSTER! #25 MOVIE CHECKLIST

MONSTER! Public Service posting: Title availability of films reviewed or mentioned in this issue of MONSTER!

Information dug up and presented by Steve Fenton and Tim Paxton.

*The Fine Print: Unless otherwise noted, all Blu-rays and DVDs listed in this section are in the NTSC Region A/Region 1 format and widescreen, as well as coming complete with English dialogue (i.e., were either originally shot in that language, or else dubbed/subbed into it). If there are any deviations from the norm, such as full-frame format, discs from different regions or foreign-language dialogue (etc.), it shall be duly noted under the headings of the individual entries below. We also include whatever related—and sometimes even totally unrelated!—ephemera/trivia which takes our fancy, and will hopefully take yours too.

BRIDES OF SODOM (2013) *[p.19]* – Streaming on Amazon from Empire Films as an Instant Video to rent ($1.99) and to buy ($4.99), in Standard Definition only.

THE CAPE CANAVERAL MONSTERS (1960) *[pp.55-76]* – As of this writing, there was a full-length rip of the film uploaded on Dailymotion (@ *http://www.dailymotion.com/ video/x22m2xr_the-cape-canaveral-monsters-1960-feature_shortfilms*). It was also on YouTube as of last year sometime, but the upload since seems to have been taken down. As of this writing, homemade DVD-Rs of **TCCM** packaged in a very crude-looking box cover were being flogged on iOffer (@ *www.ioffer.com*), though we have no idea what the picture quality of the movie is like. According to Steve B., the Italian bootleg DVD-R of **TCCM** which he mentions in his article (see jacket design on p.69) is "the finest-looking transfer of the film I've ever seen, anywhere", so until a better version comes along (if ever), it might be about the best way to go for those of us who like to watch even the lowliest of movies in the nicest available picture quality. Incidentally, the IMDb lists this title as a made-for-TV movie. If indeed that was the case, it might go far in explaining why paper promotional materials for the film have proven so difficult to come by over the decades since it was produced.

CHILDREN SHOULDN'T PLAY WITH DEAD THINGS (1972) *[p.29]* – This notorious early post-**NOTLD** zombsploitationer with the famously unforgettable run-on title was first issued on domestic DVD by VCI Home Video in the early days of Digital Versatile Disc technology (1999), in a "Restored Uncut Theatrical Version" (they also put it out on VHS, too). Even if their edition wasn't quite as fancy as they made it sound, we were glad to finally have the sucker anyway, in whatever form we could get it (Anchor Bay Entertainment also put out a version that

Makeshift cover of one of the iffy DVD-R versions available online

same year). In 2007, VCI Entertainment reissued **CSPWDT** in an "All New Film Transfer! Digitally Restored" for its "35th Anniversary Exhumed Edition". While VCI's original '99 edition was strictly no-frills/bare-bones as per usual for that budget outfit, their '07 reissue came loaded with extras, including featurettes and cast interviews. The same Exhumed Edition was subsequently reissued again (in 2010), with different packaging. In 2003, **CSPWDT** was issued as the top half of a "Bone Chilling Double Feature" DVD (two films on a single disc) by Diamond Entertainment Group (DEG), paired-up with **THE UNDERTAKER AND HIS PALS** (1966, USA, D: T.L.P. Swicegood). Australia's Umbrella Entertainment issued the former on disc Down Under in 2005, in comic book-styled cover art (complete with an "Approved by the

German DVD cover for **CHILDREN SHOULDN'T PLAY WITH DEAD THINGS**

Comics Code Authority" stamp!). Complete with an exclamation point added to the end of its title, the film was released on domestic North American Beta/VHS cassette by VidAmerica in 1989. At various other times during the '80s, it was released on domestic tape by Gorgon Video and Liberty Home Video, and it was put

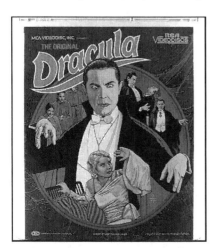

Uni's vintage early '80s RCA SelectaVision CED VideoDisc (art by Walter Velez)

out widescreen on PAL VHS tape in the UK by Exploited Film in 1999.

DRACULA (1931) *[p.107]* – Not that most *M!* readers presumably need to be told, but this iconic "Golden Age of Horror" title has been made available through Universal Pictures Home Entertainment (and its various subsidiaries/ umbrella companies) in about a trillion-gazillion different formats and editions over the decades since Uni's home movie merchandising wing Castle Films first issued it in truncated form on 8mm and 16mm film back circa the early '60s, and it—as with much of their most popular Universal Monsters series—has been available in whatever state-of-the-art medium ever since, from Regular and Super 8 on through RCA SelectaVision CED, Betamax/VHS videocassette, laserdisc, and currently on DVD and Blu-ray. You've sure come a long way, Bela! ☺

GORY GORY HALLELUJAH (2003) *[p.22]* – Evidently released on DVD just once (in 2004) by the Von Piglet Sisters/Indican Pictures, presumably in a highly limited edition.

JELLYFISH EYES (2013) *[p.45]* – Available on Blu-ray and DVD as part of The Criterion Collection. Criterion's version can also be rented/ purchased (for $3.99/$14.99) in HD only as an Amazon insta-vid.

KEPERGOK POCONG (2011) *[p.20]* – I discovered that Pinkan Utari is sometimes spelled as Pin(g)kan Utari, but the opening credits spell it without the "g". I've got one more review left in me, one involving the consumption of brains and the course of human evolution based on an Indonesian film, **MAYAT HIDUP**, but I'd love to continue with my reviews involving Indonesian horror. It's ironic that I had no intention of contributing to *Monster!* initially in its new incarnation, but now I do. However, most of the films (pre -2000) I'd like to review were once widely available on the VCD format, both as Indonesian and as Malay imports, but not so now, even online. Perhaps some kindly *M!* reader can help me locate some of these VCDs? ~ **John L. Vellutini** (The present SOV movie is uploaded to YouTube; simply key its title into the search field there, and it should be the first link that pops up. However, don't blame *Monster!* for any brain damage incurred by watching it.)

KHATRA (1991) *[p.40]* – Released on VCD by Eagle Video (#EVCD K 7448), but now apparently OOP (it is currently listed as out-of-stock at Induna [*www.induna.com*]), although it is viewable on YouTube in two parts. Also uploaded at said site is the (unrelated?) episode of India's *Zee Horror Show* also called **KHATRA**, a 90-minute feature which—as a rare bonus—comes equipped with English subtitles, unlike the present '91 film bearing the same title that's also on YT. BTW, there are literally slews of other *ZHS* features to be seen on YT, although the vast majority don't come with subs; but even if you don't happen to understand the lingo, those in any way inclined towards Indian monster/horror flicks might do well to have a browse there anyway, though.

KING OF THE ZOMBIES (1941) *[p.26]* – Adlines: *"Soulless captives of an unholy master of the Zombie cult! Condemned to live in a terrifying world of savage tortures, weird rites! ...Forced to prey upon the living and plunder the grave! LOOK – IF YOU DARE – UPON THE LIVING DEAD!"* Trailer copy: *"Abandon All Hope You Who Enter Here! For This Is the Mansion of the Walking Dead! ...Dead Men Can't Die But Live To Follow a Madman's Will – To Wreak a Voodoo Vengeance! – By the Nerve-Shuddering, Brain-Shattering Secret of the Blackest Art!"* (Can the film itself possibly even come close to living up to all that hyperbole? No, *of course* not!) "Nonsense! Zombies don't eat meat!" says the mad doctor character partway through this vintage Monogram Pictures melodrama disguised as a "horror" film... so all you dribbling gorehounds looking for some heretofore unknown *italiano* chomp'n'chowdown epic or the latest instalment to stiff-leg it off the walking dead production line, keep right on looking, cuz there's nothing to see here, so move along. Thankfully, most of the scenes following the opening set-up sequence exist purely to exploit funnyman Mantan Moreland (easily this film's most marketable commodity, in his heyday he was a highly popular comic character player with both black and white audiences; in trailers, he was billed second only to ostensible leading man Dick Purcell). A seasoned veteran of this kind of dumbness whose talents were far superior to the level of much of the material he was given, he bears the brunt of comedy relief here, but carries himself with proper professional decorum throughout. Also with dignified disdain and poise, the black butler, stereotypically and unflatteringly named "Momba" (Leigh Whipper, also seen in such classy A-list productions as Lewis Milestone's **OF MICE AND MEN** [1939] and William A. Wellman's **THE OX-BOW INCIDENT** [1943, both USA], true classics of cinematic Americana both), plays silent straight-man to Moreland. Strangely enough, although

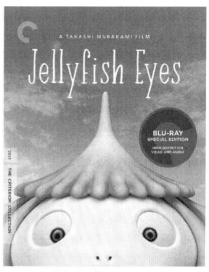

Criterion Blu-ray cover

Moreland is essentially merely playing another negative racial stereotype, due to the sheer good-humored exuberance of his delivery he comes off as far more likeable, alive and human than the rest of the cast combined, managing to carry most of the movie singlehandedly. As Moreland's character repeatedly attempts to explain to his white supposed "social superiors" (who never utter anything more than the most archetypal poverty-row Hollywood clichés), there are blank-

US DVD jacket

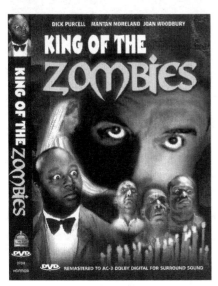

DICK PURCELL   MANTAN MORELAND   JOAN WOODBURY

KING OF THE ZOMBIES

REMASTERED TO AC-3 DOLBY DIGITAL FOR SURROUND SOUND

Front Row Entertainment's 2003 Canadian release contains a pretty decent transfer print

---

eyed zombies wandering about the island. These just happen to have been created by a native high priestess for use by Nazi-affiliated villain Dr. Mikhail Sangre (Henry "**FREAKS**" Victor), who has been working-over a captive Allied admiral using voodoo and hypnosis down in his gloomy basement in order to extract secrets for the Axis from him (don't forget, this was produced/released mere months prior the USA's active involvement in World War II). The "plot" proper never kicks in, and poorly-motivated characters go about their business in a random fashion until the final reel, which ends things in none-too-spectacular style. Amidst all this maudlin mundaneness, Moreland's easygoing mugging and smart-mouthed shtick ("This place is zombified—but *good*!") somehow have a weird dignity to them that save this half-baked excuse for a movie from becoming a speck of utter nothingness thanks to his occasional hilarious and perfectly-timed one-liners, which at times seem adlibbed on the fly and were probably all the better for it (with his spot-on comedic timing, we like to think that his directors allowed him at least a little wiggle room to improvise as he saw fit). Surprisingly enough, this minor forgotten sub-B-grade quickie actually received a '41 Academy Award nomination under the category "Scoring of a Dramatic Picture" (the composer was Edward Kay). Strange but true. Look it up if you don't believe us! This lowly, oft-dissed-and-summarily-dismissed title has been made available umpteen times on DVD since the early days of the technology, also turning up in many budget grab-

bag horror movie sets from no-name companies (presumably most of whose "masters" were pinched from the same original transfer source). Companies who have released it on DVD include Alpha Video, Navarre Entertainment, Brentwood Home Video, Mill Creek Entertainment, The Roan Group and Synergy Entertainment. One of the nicer budget editions I've seen is Front Row Entertainment's 2003 Canadian release, but there are copies of **KOTZ** of variable quality all over the net (YouTube, Dailymotion and the Internet Archive included). You'll be groaning at all this creaky old clunker's casual racism, but thankfully Moreland's comic talent transcends racial barriers and you wind up rooting for him more than for his honky sidekicks. ~ **Les Moore**

LAKE PLACID VS. ANACONDA (2015) *[p.32]* – Tagline: *"Crocs on the Dock. Snakes on the Lake."* Out on DVD from Sony Pictures Home Entertainment, and also available as an Amazon Instant Video from same (for purchase in HD only at $14.99).

LAVALANTULA (2015) *[p.37]* – Tagline: *"From SyFy, the Network that Brought You SHARKNADO"* (no shit!). Available on domestic DVD from Alchemy, this title is also up for grabs from First Look Entertainment as an Amazon insta-vid, for rental or purchase in HD mode. Be on the look-out for the inevitable insta-sequel **2 LAVA 2 LANTULA!** (2016), which should be rolling off the SyFy production line any day now (like, the day after tomorrow at latest).

LIVING HELL (2008) *[p.35]* – Under its alternate title **ORGANIZM**, Image Entertainment put it out on DVD the year of its production, in a nice wiiiiiiidescreen edition (@ a 2.35:1 aspect ratio). In Australia, it's available on DVD from Ninth Dimension Home Entertainment. For its Italian DVD release by Videa/CDE, bearing the present Anglo title but with the Italo title (**LE RADICI DEL TERRORE** / "The Roots of Terror") also given on the cover, the film came with both English and Italian dialogue options, plus soft-subs in both those languages too. Under its present title, the film should not be confused with Shūgō Fujii's Japanese splatter shocker **LIVING HELL** (生き地獄 / *Iki-jigoku*, 2000).

LONDON AFTER MIDNIGHT (1927) *[p.77]* – There are few more famed and sought-after lost Hollywood films than this one, but the odds of an intact—or even incomplete—print being discovered diminish more and more with each passing year, due to the simple fragility/perishability of the nitrate film elements involved.

However, using archival still images—including the "rare" one showing Chaney terrorizing hand-wringing Polly Moran depicted on p.82—and the script of the original intertitles, Turner Classic Movies (TCM) made a game attempt to reconstruct the film in 2002. Their reconstruction (edited by Christopher Gray), which runs 45½ minutes (sans the new end-credits), begins with an introductory word-crawl by Michael F. Blake (author of *Lon Chaney: The Man Behind the Thousand Faces* and *A Thousand Faces: Lon Chaney's Unique Artistry* [both Vestal Press, 1997], as well as *The Films of Lon Chaney* [Madison Books, 2001]), which closes with the claim, "What you are about to see is the closest possible representation of what audiences saw in movie theaters in 1927." TCM's reno-job did the best it could with the limited materials available to them, and it definitely gives us a much closer approximation of the actual film than has been seen since its original theatrical screenings, although they could only fill in the blanks just so much, so the plot's bound to be full of holes and grey areas. However, we can be thankful for the wealth of original images the re-creators dug out of the archives for the occasion. Owing more than a few obvious debts to Stoker's *Dracula* (1897), **LOF** takes a somewhat standard whodunit plotline and weaves it into what appears to be a high-Gothic horror tale concerning such things that go bump in the night as "vampyrs". Edna Tichenor as Luna, the so-called "Bat Girl" (the equivalent role more famously assumed by Carroll Borland for same director Tod Browning's talkie remake, **MARK OF THE VAMPIRE** [1935, USA]) still manages to look gore-geous (bad *FM*-style pun intended!) even with thick black eyeliner and pasty-faced pancake makeup, for that "undead" look. MGM's set designers/dressers had a field day coming up with the central old dark house setting—as the stereotypical Limey comic relief "hysterical housemaid" character played by Moran exclaims histrionically in intertitle, "'*Oly 'Enry! The bloomin' 'ouse is 'aunted!*'"—even if, for a building which has supposedly only stood empty for a mere five years rather than centuries, it certainly shows the advanced ravages of time in its dusty, decrepit and cobweb-smothered interiors, wherein slumbering bats hang from the candelabras and creepy apparitions allegedly prowl the halls in the dead of night. Even with its letdown pre-"Scooby-Doo" ending (hypnotism plays a key role in the big reveal), it's still tops on many a monster movie maven's must-see list nonetheless. The TCM reconstruction doesn't appear to have been released on disc (?), but uploads of it are viewable via such online sources as YouTube and Dailymotion, albeit broken up into multiple excerpts rather than complete. Still another attempt to reconstruct the film, this time in the print medium rather than on video, is Philip J. Riley's book *London After Midnight: A Reconstruction* (BearManor Media, 2011), which features a foreword by the late Forrest J. Ackerman. Also of definite interest is editor Niels W. Erickson's recent reprint (by Couch Pumpkin Classics/*lulu.com*, 2012) of Marie Coolidge-Rask's original tie-in novelization (originally published in 1928 by Grosset & Dunlap of NYC), which was based on Browning's own screenplay.

THE LORELEY'S GRASP (1973) *[p.9]* – Deimos Entertainment released a real sweet domestic DVD edition in 2007, which is now out-of-print, as the company is no more. That same year, BCI/Eclipse issued a widescreen (1.85:1) DVD edition, "Mastered in High Definition from the Original Negative". BCI also released it in alternate packaging as part of their "Spanish Horror Collection", which also included other key Amando de Ossorio and Paul Naschy titles. In 2012, under the present Anglo export title (with the German alternate title **DIE BESTIE IM MÄDCHEN-PENSIONAT** ["The Beast in the Girls' Boarding School"] also given on the cover), it was put out in Germany on PAL Region 2 DVD by ELEA-Media in a Limited Collector's Edition of just 2000 copies. Nice thing about this release is, it came not only with German/Spanish dialogue options, but also with an English audio

US VHS cover

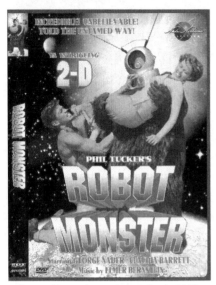

Image Entertainment's just-dandy 2000 DVD edition

domestic Blu-ray/DVD combo edition, which comes with an unbelievably sumptuous transfer print that can only make this lowly exploitation entry look that much better than ever before (we doubt if most original theatrical screenings even looked as nice as this disc does!). In 2007, grey-market outfit Videoasia put it out on DVD as part of their "Grindhouse Experience" series, in what was presumably merely a copy of an old VHS version (?). Speaking of which, it had been put out on British PAL Beta/VHS tape by Worldwide Entertainment Corporation in 1982, and the following year Media Home Entertainment issued it on domestic NTSC videocassette. Under the compound title **RAWFORCE** *[sic]*, it was issued on '80s Beta/VHS tape in Norway by VCL, with its original English audio track and Norwegian subtitles. You'd never guess there were zombies in it judging by VCL's cover art, but there's a crudely-rendered bound-and-gagged topless chick on the front that probably got more than a few horny modern Vikings' attention back in the day.

track as well. Hence, those who can't find a copy of the now-*kaput* Deimos' edition and who have an All-Region player might like to opt for the German edition instead.

RAW FORCE (1982) *[p.17]* – UK ad-lines: *"It's* [sic] *nourishment – human flesh... It's* [sic] *guardian – the undead... It's* [sic] *sanctuary – the island."* The version to beat for now and possibly all time is Vinegar Syndrome's 2014

SALEM'S LOT artwork by Andy Ross

ROBOT MONSTER (1953) *[p.55]* – Image Entertainment's welcome year 2000 domestic DVD release of **RM** as part of their Wade Williams Collection (*"In Intriguing 2-D"*) contains a pretty pristine print, which was specially remastered for this IE edition, and looks about as good as you'd expect a film of this vintage to look after so many intervening decades. Other than that and a movie trailer for the film, that's all she wrote, but the niceness of the transfer print more than makes up for the dearth of extras. Just for the record, an inevitable *Mystery Science Theater 3000* fuck-with has also been released. Copies of both the "straight" original and *MST3K*'s version are on YouTube. Which one will *you* choose...?

SALEM'S LOT (1979) *[p.3]* – As **SALEM'S LOT: THE MOVIE**, the original more-than-three-hour miniseries was released in a 112-minute edit on domestic Beta/VHS cassette in 1984 by Warner Home Video, and then again in 1987. Warners, who've kept a firm hold on the franchise over the years, also released Larry Cohen's belated "sequel", **A RETURN TO SALEM'S LOT** (1987, USA), as well as Turner Network Television (TNT)'s 2004 remake of the originating film, too.

SON OF INGAGI (1940) *[p.48]* – This long-unseen title was initially rediscovered and put out on home videocassette back in the '80s by the venerable Sinister Cinema. Also in the USA, both J&J Video and Madhouse Video apparently put it out on VHS tape in 2004, around the same time that Echo Bridge Entertainment and Alpha Video Distributors each put it out on DVD. The Internet Archive (*www.archive.org*) has a pretty "okay" copy of this long-PD title up for view and/ or download, but, like most (all?) other extant versions, it appears to be missing the better part of ten minutes of footage; this evidently not due to censorial cuts but simply as a result of severe physical damage. Scrappy, choppy copies are also viewable on both YouTube and Dailymotion. Those who really want to see this quaintly archaic relic of "race cinema" won't mind putting up with the less-than-optimal condition, though.

UNDER THE BLOSSOMING CHERRY TREES (1975) *[p.24]* – Currently streaming on Amazon for either rental ($2.99) or purchase ($4.99), in the SD format only. It was originally issued on Japanese videocassette during the '80s and '90s by Toho Video, who also put it out on Japanese DVD in 2005.

WENDIGO: BOUND BY BLOOD (2010) *[p.34]* – Under the title **BOUND BY BLOOD: WENDIGO**, this is listed on Amazon as an insta-vid, although as of this writing it was unavailable either for rental or purchase. It has been included in at least one horror movie DVD set from Echo Bridge Home Entertainment, though.

Who would ever guess what horrors lurk behind this Japanese DVD cover for **UNDER THE BLOSSOMING CHERRY TREES**

Rare pressbook art for the equally obscure film

Chuck Jarman of Bump In The Night FX put this bust he made of **CSPWDT**'s Orville up for auction on eBay in 2011

117

30408927R00074

Made in the USA
San Bernardino, CA
13 February 2016